C000092400

HOLISTIC SPACES

HOLISTIC SPACES

108 WAYS TO CREATE A MINDFUL AND PEACEFUL HOME

anjie cho

CICO BOOKS

LONDON NEW YORK

DEDICATION

This book is dedicated to my mother and father.

Thank you for creating safe, loving, and nurturing spaces
for me throughout my entire life.

Published in 2018 by CICO Books
An imprint of Ryland Peters & Small Ltd
20–21 Jockey's Fields   341 E 116th St
London WC1R 4BW   New York, NY 10029

www.rylandpeters.com

10 9 8 7 6 5 4 3 2

Text © Anjie Cho 2018
Design © CICO Books 2018
Photography © Ryland Peters & Small Ltd and
CICO Books 2018

The author's moral rights have been asserted. All
rights reserved. No part of this publication may
be reproduced, stored in a retrieval system, or
transmitted in any form or by any means, electronic,
mechanical, photocopying, or otherwise, without
the prior permission of the publisher.

A CIP catalog record for this book is available
from the Library of Congress and the British
Library.

ISBN: 978-1-78249-667-0

Printed in China

Photography: full credits can be found
on page 175
Illustrator: (Chippy) Heung-Heung Chin

Commissioning editor: Kristine Pidkameny
In-house editor: Anna Galkina
Art director: Sally Powell
Production controller: David Hearn
Publishing manager: Penny Craig
Publisher: Cindy Richards

CONTENTS

foreword

Anjie Cho's *Holistic Spaces* shows a new direction in providing simple help to implement the benefits and blessings of feng shui and green design. If you follow her suggestions, you will create spaces in your home and workplace that support your dreams and advance your life.

When I was a child in the 1960s, feng shui was virtually unknown in the West. Even in China, many rejected this profound art and science as superstition. As the first person to teach and consult in feng shui in the West (even before my master, His Holiness Professor Thomas Lin Yun, Da Shih, a living Buddha, came to the United States and opened the roads for feng shui to be an international force), I have seen interest grow from a trickle to a torrent. My childhood dream of understanding and using the unity of person, place, and universe to help mankind has become a reality. Professor Lin Yun asked me and two colleagues to create a professional education program to train skilled practitioners to benefit society. This three-year program, of which my friend and student, the eminent architect Anjie Cho, is a graduate, continues as the BTB Feng Shui Masters Training Program in New York City in partnership with the New York Open Center. It is the only program of its type to have state accreditation.

Of my many students, Anjie Cho is one of the most gifted. I have known Anjie since 2010, and in the eight years since then, she has earned my respect as a student able to bring feng shui knowledge into accord with modern architectural practice and green design to advance her ideal of holistic feng shui.

I knew that Anjie's book would be of high quality and relevance even before she asked me to read the text, make suggestions, and write this foreword.

I have witnessed her interest, application, long-term study, respect for the tradition, ongoing commitment to self-improvement and gaining knowledge, and kindness and wish to help the world. Each of these is an important characteristic of a good feng shui consultant. Anjie has attended many consultations with me both as a student and after she graduated the masters program. She has provided excellent analysis and suggestions for residences, businesses, and localities, drawing upon her broad studies in architecture and green design and on the feng shui knowledge that she shares so cogently in this book.

In the first part of her book, Anjie presents key concepts and applications of the feng shui bagua map, also known as the ever-changing eight trigrams. In an easy-to-understand format, she provides many concepts, techniques, and tools for transforming and improving environments, including how to use colors most effectively. She draws upon her knowledge of the method of minor additions, selecting the easiest and most effective ways of applying light, life, color, five element theory, and more in a way that is truly easy to integrate with how people now live and work. She includes secrets of the "commanding position," and describes the power of intention to allow you to position yourself for success and to bring both visible and invisible forces to support your life. She also includes simple and effective methods of space clearing to cleanse and invigorate your home or office.

In the second part of the book, Anjie shares how to create an inviting entry to receive what the world brings to you. She also conveys how to create a lively and entertaining living room to support life's pleasures and comforts. She imparts how to create a kitchen that will nourish you at many levels, including contributing to your advancement in the world, and conveys how your dining room can best support satisfaction in eating and also connect family members and friends. She explains how to skillfully set up a home office, coordinating practical aspects of feng shui and green design. She shares bathroom basics and techniques for both protecting your wealth and making your bathroom friendly to the environment. She also offers good advice and best practices to make your bedroom a fortress of comfort and repose. Her discussion of this important influence on our lives includes examining how to select the right bed and what you need to know to make your bedroom nurturing, supportive, and encouraging of a wish-fulfilling life.

Anjie also discusses where best to meditate, the meaning and best use of closets, the role of plants, and how to understand and employ doors and windows, the mouth and eyes of your home, including how to correct some difficult door and window situations so that what once may have created a life problem is transformed into an uplifting and supportive environmental factor.

Holistic Spaces concludes with a section on how nine minutes a day of feng shui maintenance, support, and activity can help you easily move toward your goals.

Let Anjie take you by the hand and lead you on a path of learning and self-improvement in correctly and creatively adjusting your environment. I encourage those who open this book to read it thoroughly, think about what is presented, and implement the suggestions. You will bring the blessings of holistic feng shui and green design into true effectiveness. Starting with yourself, advance on this true path toward a better life for yourself and the world.

Steven Post
Geomancy/Feng Shui Education Association
Author of *The Modern Book of Feng Shui*

introduction

What are holistic spaces? Holistic spaces are designed by looking beyond the surface to create awareness and an environment that supports and nurtures the inhabitants. Holistic design seeks to create spaces that resonate from both the inside and the outside—from your spirit, your body, your home, the planet, and the universe as a whole.

In creating holistic spaces, I combine many different disciplines, including feng shui, green design, Buddhist and Taoist philosophies, and environmental psychology. Similar to meditation, feng shui is about mindfulness in our everyday lives. It's about looking at all the details around us, the mundane as much as the fascinating parts. When we are present for every moment, we can see the beauty and magic in our spaces.

I like to say that feng shui is the original "green design." Through observing and shifting the built environment, feng shui teaches us how to live in harmony with nature. Eco-friendly design looks at your own personal health and also how human actions impact nature and the earth. Feng shui looks at the same issues: how does the environment affect us on an energetic level and, in turn, how do we influence the planet as a whole?

Feng shui is an ancient Asian art of placement developed thousands of years ago. Feng shui seeks to enhance and improve the flow of energy through your environment, to maximize the positive potential for your life. A truly holistic way to look at your environment, it may include interior or architectural design, but it's really more than that. Feng shui looks beyond the superficial and is about creating awareness beyond what you see on the surface. The intent is to create an environment that nourishes you holistically.

Feng shui adjustments can bring balance to your home because the principles are founded upon cycles and patterns of nature and ancient knowledge. Sadly, many of us have lost touch with this knowledge. Feng shui can teach us to be in tune with our environment and aware of how we impact the earth, as well as how it affects us.

I primarily practice BTB feng shui, which is one of the many schools of feng shui. I find that BTB feng shui is more relevant for me and my clients as Westerners, because it focuses on intention to empower the adjustments and the flow of qi rather than a compass direction. I feel this is more compatible for us because we are not living in ancient China. Therefore, most of the suggestions in this book are based on the BTB feng shui philosophy.

As a holistic interior architect, I encounter many people who wish to integrate feng shui and eco-friendly design into their homes and businesses, but they want to wait until the space is clean, or until they have more time, or until they move. These are, of course, appropriate times to renovate or redecorate, but what most people don't know is that you can incorporate feng shui and green-living principles at any time. It may be even more helpful at a challenging time. This is about more than just moving furniture around; it's about shifting your environment physically and energetically to support your life. Even if you are not ready to renovate or redesign your home, you can still incorporate holistic principles into your space.

Feng shui can be simple and straightforward. Take some time and look at how you can rearrange your lifestyle and position yourself in command of your present to encourage relaxation and allow the best of you to shine through. Recognize that you are actively making a small change to let the universe know you are ready to accept the best things that are coming to you.

getting started

You can use this book as a reference guide, or simply read one of the tips each day. Remember that this is not about seeing dramatic results. Instead it is about amassing small shifts and noticing the subtle changes that happen. Please take time and delight in the simple shifts in your environment as well as your perceptions. Feng shui and green lifestyle changes can influence mindfulness in all aspects of your life.

Remember, this is just the tip of the iceberg when it comes to creating holistic spaces. I'm sharing simple and effective tools to help you begin to make shifts on an environmental level. To truly take the holistic approach, open up your awareness. I encourage you to go beyond your space and make personal, social, universal transformations.

My aspiration is that each of my readers begins to make some shifts to create harmonious living and work spaces to support and nurture healthy and conscious lives.

THE FENG SHUI BAGUA MAP

how to lay the bagua

TO USE THE FENG SHUI BAGUA MAP TO THE RIGHT, PLEASE ALIGN THE BOTTOM OF THE MAP WITH THE ENTRANCE WALL OF YOUR SPACE (THE WALL THAT CONTAINS YOUR DOOR). Stand in the doorway of your home, office, or any room and face into the space. Divide the room in a 3x3 grid. You will be standing in the Knowledge, Path in Life, or Benefactors area. The Abundance area is in the far back left corner, and the Relationships area is in the far back right corner.

The bagua is one of the most important aspects of feng shui, as it assists in determining which parts of your space relate to each specific type of energy. Without defining this correctly, you cannot properly execute feng shui. Look into which bagua area relates to an area that you need to work on, and get started!

Note: This is my simplified version of the Feng Shui Bagua Map. Each of these areas can expand to relate to every aspect of your life. You may feel the urge to correct them all, but please remember not to make this about perfection. My teachers taught me to only work on the areas that need attention. Be kind to yourself and choose the three or so areas that you can truly and honestly work on with your best effort.

ABUNDANCE	RECOGNITION	RELATIONSHIPS
purple yin wood 4 *wealth* *xun*	red fire 9 *reputation* summer *li*	pink yin earth 2 *partners* *kun*

NEW BEGINNINGS	HEALTH	COMPLETION
blue-green yang wood 3 *family* spring *zhen*	yellow-orange-brown earth 5 *center* *tai qi*	white yin metal 7 *joy* fall *dui*

KNOWLEDGE	PATH IN LIFE	BENEFACTORS
dark blue yang earth 8 *self-cultivation* *gen*	black water 1 *career* winter *kan*	gray yang metal 6 *travel* *qian*

ALIGN WITH ENTRANCE WALL OF YOUR SPACE

tip 2

This modern living wall garden can bring in the vibrant energy to the new beginnings area of your home. The verticality can also uplift the qi in the space.

new beginnings
WHERE WE ALWAYS BEGIN

IN FENG SHUI WE OFTEN START WITH THE NEW BEGINNINGS AREA OF THE BAGUA OF THE HOME, ZHEN, WHICH IS RELATED TO NEW BEGINNINGS OF ANY KIND—CREATION, FAMILY MATTERS, AND THE SEASON AND ENERGY OF SPRING—AND IS SYMBOLIZED BY THE COLOR BLUE-GREEN, THE NUMBER THREE, COLUMNAR AND TALL SHAPES, AND THE ELEMENT OF YANG WOOD. It has that magnificent burst of energy associated with a sprout pushing out of the ground and the excitement of the first beautifully sunny and warm day of spring.

This is a great area to work with if you have trouble starting new things. You may also choose to activate this area if you need support in new projects or more harmony in your family.

As the first way to create holistic space, please take some time and place something meaningful in this area to symbolize a new start to creating a healing and organic home. A green plant or water fountain may be especially effective in this area to inspire growth and the nourishment that you need to heal.

abundance

OVERFLOWING FULLNESS

THE ABUNDANCE AREA OF THE FENG SHUI BAGUA, CALLED XUN, IS RELATED TO WEALTH, ABUNDANCE, PROSPERITY, AND SELF-WORTH, REPRESENTED BY THE COLOR PURPLE, THE NUMBER FOUR, COLUMNAR AND TALL SHAPES, AND THE ELEMENT OF YIN WOOD. Yin wood energy is like a big tree grounded with deep roots and a large canopy.

This is one of the most popular areas of the bagua. It is not just about money, though. Your wealth in the world is dependent on and related to your self-worth, so this area is also about having an abundance of the positive aspects in your life.

What is going on in the Abundance areas of your home, particularly in your bedroom and office? Take some time and place something meaningful in these areas of your bedroom and/or office. If you need some stability in your finances, try a heavy statue. If you need more cash flow, a water fountain may be especially effective in this area.

A heavy object, such as this Buddha statue or a large rock, can ground and give stability to your wealth, abundance, and self-worth. It's like the roots of a tree finding nourishment in the earth. This Buddha is sitting firmly supported on the earth.

There are countless ways that one can invoke the earth element of the health area with square shapes and earthy tones such as yellow, many of which can be seen in the example above. The flowering yellow plant also adds the element of kindness and gives life to your health area.

health THE CENTER OF YOUR HOME

THE HEALTH AREA OF THE FENG SHUI BAGUA IS CALLED TAI QI, WHICH IS RELATED TO YOUR OVERALL HEALTH, SIGNIFIED BY EARTHY COLORS (YELLOW, ORANGE, BROWN), THE NUMBER FIVE, SQUARE OR FLAT SHAPES, AND THE ELEMENT OF EARTH. If you look at the location of this area, it is in the center. The energy of the center affects physical, mental, and emotional health.

The health area is in the center because it affects and is influenced by all eight bagua areas around it. This central area touches all aspects of your life, so of course it influences your health and well-being.

A great way to support your overall health is to activate the tai qi of your home. A yellow-toned square rug in the center of your bedroom, living room, or home provides centralized stability and helps to create interconnectedness with people and the various aspects of your life.

benefactors ASSISTANCE FROM THE HEAVENS

THE BENEFACTORS AREA OF THE FENG SHUI
BAGUA IS CALLED QIAN, WHICH IS RELATED TO
HELPFUL PEOPLE, BENEFACTORS, THE ENERGY
OF HEAVEN, TRAVEL, AND THE FATHER, ALL
SYMBOLIZED BY THE COLOR GRAY, THE NUMBER
SIX, CIRCULAR SHAPES, AND THE ELEMENT OF
YANG METAL, LIKE SHINY JEWELRY.

Often we need help from others, whether that
be people or the heavens, to move forward.
Adjustments can be made in this area to bring
supportive energy and people into your life.

If you need some support, place a metal wind
chime in this area of your home. When the
chimes ring, the sound will let the world know
that you need support. You can also try a large
piece of pyrite or labradorite in this area. Pyrite
brings in more fatherly energy and protection,
giving you support. Labradorite attracts
heavenly energy to connect you to the universe.
These crystals from the earth support the metal
element of the Benefactors area.

The bright reflective qualities of silver and gold, as well as the melodic
tinkling sounds of metal chimes can wake us up! Hanging metal chimes in
the benefactors area creates vibrations that resonate throughout your
home and into the world with your intentions and wishes. When placed in
the kitchen, metal chimes can activate the energy of helpful people in
consideration of your wealth and nourishment.

tip 6

completion CHILDREN OF ALL KINDS

THE COMPLETION AREA OF THE FENG SHUI BAGUA IS CALLED DUI, WHICH IS RELATED TO COMPLETION, CHILDREN, ANY SORT OF OUTPUT OR OFFSPRING, JOY, AND THE SEASON AND ENERGY OF FALL. The color white, the number seven, circular shapes, and the element of yin metal, like unrefined metal ore within the earth's core, relate to Completion.

Completion is about closure and the end of things. But ends bring new beginnings. This area would be great to activate if you have trouble completing projects.

This area is also about joy. A great way to bring joy into your life is to keep fresh flowers in the completion areas of your bedroom, living roo,m and entry. The fragrance of flowers is transformative and brings life energy into your space. Fresh flowers are also excellent at "un-sticking" things that are "stuck." Get that joy and qi flowing!

Bouquets of flowers in the completion area bring joy and celebration. White flowers echo the color, and the metal vase the element of the completion area. If possible, pick wild flowers if you can to create a stronger result.

knowledge SELF-KNOWLEDGE AND CULTIVATION

THE KNOWLEDGE AREA OF THE FENG SHUI
BAGUA IS CALLED GEN, WHICH IS RELATED TO
KNOWLEDGE AND SELF-CULTIVATION AND IS
REPRESENTED BY THE COLOR DARK BLUE, THE
NUMBER EIGHT, SQUARE AND FLAT SHAPES,
AND THE ELEMENT OF YANG EARTH, LIKE A
BIG MOUNTAIN YOU MIGHT CLIMB TO MEDITATE
AT THE APEX.

This area is about your spiritual inclination
to grow and develop your inner life. It's
also about your level of skill and wisdom in
mundane areas of your life such as your career.

The Knowledge area is a great place for
your library, books, and/or a meditation space.
Reading books can educate you and help to
improve your proficiency and skillfulness in all
areas of your life. Similarly, meditation assists
in your spiritual development. These activities
may be doubly effective if done with clear
intention in your Knowledge area.

This deep, dark blue, almost black, bookshelf is the
color of the knowledge area. Gather books here
that inspire you, that teach you, and that make your
heart sing!

tip 8

A green plant in the recognition area of the bedroom can get you noticed and create inspiration in your life. Flowering plants even more so!

recognition FAME AND PASSION

THE RECOGNITION AREA OF THE FENG SHUI BAGUA IS CALLED LI, WHICH IS RELATED TO FAME, PASSION, RECOGNITION, REPUTATION, AND THE SEASON AND ENERGY OF SUMMER. The color red, the number nine, triangular shapes, and the element of fire symbolize the Recognition area.

Pay attention to this area if you want to be seen and recognized. It influences and improves your level of passion and how the world sees you. It is a great area to activate if you are starting any new endeavors that require public support.

If you need more recognition in your life, at work or in your relationships, try placing a plant in this area of your desk (for work) or bedroom (for relationships). The wood of the plant will feed and cultivate the fire of Recognition.

path in life THE STEPS YOU TAKE

THE PATH IN LIFE AREA OF THE FENG SHUI BAGUA
IS CALLED KAN, WHICH IS RELATED TO YOUR
CAREER AS WELL AS THE SEASON AND ENERGY OF
WINTER. The color black, the number one, wavy
shapes, and the element of water symbolize
this area.

This is the path you walk in life, and how you
express your efforts in the world. It does not
necessarily have to be a traditional career, but
it pertains to how you move through the course
of your life.

If you need some more support in your career
you could do some adjustments in this area of
your home or office. A water fountain with the
flow of water directed toward the center of the
space is ideal. This will also encourage cash
flow for the inhabitants if placed near the entry
of the home.

If the entry of your home is in the Path in Life bagua
area, a black accent wall can attract and absorb
career opportunities.

Rose quartz and the relationship area both embody love and self-love. A pair is suggested for relationships, but sometimes what you really need is just one because to truly find a partner, you must find true compassion and love for yourself.

kun RELATIONSHIPS

THE RELATIONSHIPS AREA OF THE FENG SHUI BAGUA IS CALLED KUN, WHICH IS RELATED TO RELATIONSHIPS, PARTNERSHIPS, THE MOTHER, AND MARRIAGE, AND SYMBOLIZED BY THE COLOR PINK, THE NUMBER TWO, SQUARE AND FLAT SHAPES, AND THE ELEMENT OF YIN EARTH, LIKE SAND ON A BEACH.

This area is probably the second most popular because it can activate attracting a primary relationship. But relationships can also refer to business partnerships or other important connections in your life.

If you are looking to attract a romantic partner, this is the area to work on. It is best to work on the Relationships area in your bedroom, which represents you and also your future partner. One powerful adjustment is to select two pieces of tumbled rose quartz and place them in the Relationships area of your bedroom. If you already have a partner, you can place two live bamboo stalks in a single vase to represent steady growth in your relationship.

FENG SHUI COLORS

tip 11

The colors of fall leaves—earthy browns and yellows, conjure up emotions that we can all relate to immediately. We feel the poignancy of the end of summer and beginning of fall. Colors can influence our moods immediately.

how to approach colors

COLORS ARE ONE OF THE BASIC WAYS TO ADJUST YOUR FENG SHUI. Humans rely heavily on visuals to adapt to the world around them; therefore, color has a huge influence on how we relate to our moods, healing, and emotions. Color is light, in varying wavelengths. So why not use color to shift your energy?

In nature, color defines the seasons. Winter is dark and white. In spring things begin to sprout green. Summer is bright and sunny and full of vibrant colors. In the fall, the leaves begin to turn yellow and brown. Colors in our environment also indicate the time of day. At dawn colors are soft and muted, at noon colors are vibrant with the intensity of the sunlight, and colors darken as night approaches.

With colors, we also have our own personal cultural conditioning. Our associations with colors depend a lot on where we live. For example, in China, traditionally white is worn to funerals and black to weddings. In the West, it is the opposite. Colors also stimulate nostalgia. Some colors can resonate with particular memories. Whether a color is related to your memory or your cultural conditioning, pay attention to your reactions to colors. Be sure to explore your personal associations and honor them.

hopeful greens and blues

GREENS, TEALS, AND BLUES ARE ASSOCIATED WITH
HOPE, NEW BEGINNINGS, AND GROWTH, LIKE
PLANTS AND THE ELEMENT OF WOOD. These colors
are calming and relaxing, and lend themselves
to tranquility and healthy supportive energy.
These are balancing colors and the colors of
nature and plants.

In feng shui, green and blue represent life and
renewed energy and activate the area of New
Beginnings. These two colors can be extremely
restorative. Bright fluorescent colors are more
stimulating and refreshing. Green is related to the
heart chakra, which is related to emotional healing
and empathy.

Greens and blues are great to use as wall paint
colors for most rooms in a home. Soft hues are
especially beneficial in the bedroom when one
needs rest. In more public rooms where we
entertain, the stronger tones of blue and green,
especially teal, can promote conversation and
enliven the room.

Placement of green plants (living or fake) also
promotes growth and healing in the home. Jade
is a wonderfully healing stone you can use in
the New Beginnings area of your bedroom to
reinforce self-healing.

The vibrant blues, teals, and greens in this palette are
perfect in a living room to invigorate and refresh.

Elegant purple flowers in a vase in the Abundance area of your desk invites prosperity into your career.

elegant purples and violets

PURPLE IS AN AUSPICIOUS FENG SHUI COLOR CONNECTED WITH WEALTH AND ABUNDANCE, AND OFTEN ASSOCIATED WITH ELEGANCE AND ROYALTY. Purple is the combination of fiery red and relaxing blue. Therefore, this color can harmonize and create inner balance and peace.

Purple is also the color of the crown chakra, which is related to enlightenment and wisdom. This color can be used to activate the Abundance area of your desk, bedroom, or home to attract more wealth and self-worth into your life.

Amethyst is a beautiful crystal that can be placed in your Abundance area to invite prosperity and nobility into your home. Pale and deep violets can be calming and balancing. Purple flowers or accents may also be used in the Abundance area.

earthy yellows, oranges, and browns

THE COLORS YELLOW, ORANGE, AND BROWN
ARE RADIANT, WARM, AND FREQUENTLY FOUND
IN NATURE. They are also the colors of the
harvest season, which can symbolize both
activity and hibernation.

Deep earthy shades indicate strength and
endurance, while also being nurturing and
tranquil. Thr pale browns and neutral tones of
sand and soil are soothing hues, representing
stability and the nurturing of mother earth.
Brown can be elegant and also symbolize
the quiet steadiness of a tree. For a calm
atmosphere, stay on the light end, but away
from yellow colors. Flesh tones are appropriate
for restful rooms such as the bedroom.

On the other end of the spectrum are the
stimulating tones of orange and yellow. Bright
yellows and oranges are longer wavelengths
and can stimulate appetite. The brighter hues
may be supportive for the center of the home
to activate the Health area of the bagua.

The restful earthy hues in this bedroom invite
you to hibernate and be cozy. The deep, warm
orange and brown tones in the wooden headboard,
pillows, and blankets invoke the earth element
of nourishment and self-care.

An all-white room with the warmth of a light wood floor can accentuate the qualities of precision and simplicity. White always brightens up a space, reflecting the most light.

complementary whites

WHITE SYMBOLIZES PURITY, HEAVEN, AND SIMPLICITY. WHITE IS THE ABSENCE OF ALL COLOR AND CAN REPRESENT A BLANK SLATE. In nature, we see white in clouds and snow. Clouds refer to the heavens, while the winter snow reminds us of stark coldness. White is the ultimate yang, or active, color.

White is a great base to start with, but it's best to avoid creating rooms that are entirely stark white. White can be sharp and harsh on the eyes. Imagine walking in a field of snow; it is glaringly blinding and exhausting. Our eyes see white as a brilliant color.

I personally love mostly white rooms, but there are so many shades of white. Off-whites are softer and friendlier. You can combine creamy or warmer off-whites to create an all-white room. Of course, another option is to use white to contrast other colors. I do recommend a pure white paint color for ceilings in a flat finish, as this reflects the most light into a room, creating the appearance of a larger, brighter, and lighter space.

There is a Buddhist adage regarding teacups. Full cup, cup with a hole, upside-down cup, or an open empty cup, which one are you? If you are an empty cup, you may receive help and support from those around you.

supportive and neutral grays

GRAYS ARE CONSIDERED TRANQUIL AND QUIET, AS THEY ARE A BALANCE OF BLACK AND WHITE, YIN AND YANG. They are also neutral shades that can complement almost any color. Gray can feel a bit cold, depressing, and isolating, reminiscent of being stuck inside on a rainy day. Gray is thought of as an ambiguous color, as in the "gray area."

Because it is such a noncommittal color, grayish hues are suitable for most spaces. Simply use them in combination with any other color to generate a more sophisticated and supported look.

Gray is also related to the area of Benefactors, which attracts helpful people. In addition, grays are helpful in supporting the intention of the other colors you use in a particular space.

This embroidered indigo lamp shade is reminiscent of a starry night. You can imagine you're sprawled out in the middle of nowhere staring at the stars, connecting to your inner wisdom. The deep shades of dark blue create a sense of calm.

deep and dark blues

DARK BLUES ARE RELATED TO THE CONTEMPLATIVE KNOWLEDGE AREA OF THE BAGUA. Deep hues of blue create a meditative feeling of exhaling, which relaxes tensions and refreshes the body. Blue tones can provide a sense of security and calm.

In nature we see dark blues in the night sky or when peering down into the deep ocean. Blues give an overall quiet and settled feeling, especially dark blues.

This color also governs the throat chakra, which is the gateway through which we communicate and express ourselves. Lapis lazuli is a blue stone that assists in opening up the throat chakra, and supports self-expression and growth. A piece of this crystal is especially supportive if placed in the Knowledge or Completion area of your bedroom or meditation area.

fiery reds

RED IS THE MOST AUSPICIOUS COLOR WHEN IT COMES TO
FENG SHUI. It is sensuous, dynamic, and very stimulating.
While red is appropriate for many applications, it is not
suitable for relaxing environments because it can be very
active. Take care to use it in moderation, as a little bit of
red can go a long way.

It makes perfect sense that red is also associated with fire,
passion, and the Recognition area of the bagua.

If you need some more passion in the bedroom, add
some red sheets or a red blanket. Buying some new sexy red
underwear will also help. If you are looking for a promotion
or some recognition in your career, try placing a Mars yantra
in the Recognition area of your home office or desk. A
yantra is a Tantric mandala composed of interlocking
geometric figures—such as circles, triangles, and floral
shapes—that form a pattern. They can be used to
strengthen your meditative focus. By using a red yantra,
you can adjust lack of passion and fame by adding fire.

This door is painted in black chalkboard paint, which creates drama when paired with a white wall. The chalkboard paint invites you to share your story, and give that door a voice. Doors represent the voices of a home's inhabitants.

wise blacks

IN FENG SHUI, BLACK IS RELATED TO WISDOM AND KNOWLEDGE. BLACK IS THE COMBINATION OF ALL COLORS. It has depth and symbolizes the incorporation of all things. Black is also the most yin or passive color.

Although black can be contemplative, too much will generate a dark look. Excessive black is not appropriate for home interiors because it will absorb light and feel oppressive and depressing. Instead, blacks can be used as dramatic accent pieces.

Because black absorbs, black tourmaline is excellent for protection from negative energy, including electromagnetic smog. Use four pieces to create a grid under your bed, in your bedroom, or for your entire home. Place one piece in each corner (of the bed, bedroom, or entire home). This generates an energetic grid of security and absorbs most types of harmful energy.

These rosy hues are perfect to attract love and partnership into your life. You can bring in pink with paint, linens, or pillows, and wearing pink is especially effective.

romantic pinks and "peach blossom luck"

PINKS AND PEACH TONES ARE CONNECTED TO THE RELATIONSHIP AREA OF THE FENG SHUI MAP. These colors are feminine, nurturing, romantic, soft, and innocent. Pink is also associated with youthfulness, love, and joy.

Pink and peach colors, especially on painted walls, are incredibly flattering for skin tones. You will be seen through "rose-colored glasses" in a pink setting. The color makes you appear healthier and creates a glow.

In feng shui, peach is a very lucky color for attracting a romantic partner. We call it "peach blossom luck." It is ideal to paint your bedroom peach and wear peach to attract your future mate. After you meet the right person, be sure to change the intention of the paint color to support the new relationship rather than attracting a new one!

FIVE ELEMENT THEORY

how to use five element theory

IN FENG SHUI, WE EMPLOY FIVE ELEMENT THEORY, A PHILOSOPHY USED TO DESCRIBE
THE CYCLES OF NATURE AND HOW THEY WORK TOGETHER AND SEEK TO ALWAYS
BE IN BALANCE. The five elements are earth, water, fire, wood, and metal. Five
element theory is also utilized in traditional Chinese medicine, Chinese astrology,
and martial arts.

The five elements can be used in a "creation" or "overcoming" sequence to
produce or reduce an imbalance of a particular element. For instance, if you need
more fire, you can add more wood, which produces fire. Alternatively, if you have
too much fire, you might add water, which reduces the flames of a fire.

A great and simple way to create balance and harmony is to include something
that represents each of these five elements in your space. You can do this by
adding colors, materials, or shapes that correspond to each of the elements as
described in the following tips.

earth

THE ELEMENT OF EARTH IS RELATED TO EARTHY COLORS LIKE
BROWN, ORANGE, OR YELLOW AND THE FENG SHUI BAGUA
AREAS OF RELATIONSHIPS, HEALTH, AND KNOWLEDGE. Earth
also has the qualities of stability and nourishment, like
mother earth. The earth element creates metal, because
metal ores come from the earth's core. Earth overcomes
water, as the banks of a river control the direction of the flow
and because soil can muddy water.

You may have too much earth if you care too much
for others without first taking care of yourself. For this
imbalance you can add metal, which depletes earth, or
wood, which breaks up earth. If you are very self-centered,
selfish, and care for no one but yourself, you may have too
little earth. For this imbalance you can add earth or fire,
which produces earth. When earth is balanced you take care
of yourself first, which allows you to truly care for others.

Some examples of earth are objects with a square shape;
orange, brown, or yellow colors; or composition from the
earth, such as a large stone sculpture. You can add the earth
element with a stone statue or large natural stone such as
jasper, which is heavy and from the earth, providing stability
and support. A big wooden desk is also earth element, as it
is brown, earthy in color, squarish, and has weight to it.

Although you might think that a
wooden desk represents the wood
element, it's really more earth.
A heavy, brown wooden desk like
this can ground and stabilize
your career.

water

THE ELEMENT OF WATER IS RELATED TO DARK COLORS, LIKE BLACK AND VERY DARK BLUE, AND THE FENG SHUI BAGUA AREA OF PATH IN LIFE. Water has the qualities of fluidity, wisdom, and intelligence. It is also related to your social network and how you interact with the world. The water element creates wood, because water supports plants and trees as well as all life. Water overcomes fire, as it extinguishes the flames.

You may have too much water if you are overwhelmed with social activities and spread yourself too thin. For this imbalance you can add earth, which muddies water, or wood, which depletes water. If you are isolated, with problems connecting with others and finding opportunities, you may have too little water. For this imbalance you can add water or metal, which generates water. When water is balanced, you connect with the outside world, and it responds to you in a balanced manner where you receive appropriate connections and opportunities.

Water items include wavy shapes and, of course, anything with actual water. A water fountain or fish tank are both simple and beautiful ways to add water to your space. Mirrors support the water element and can visually expand your space. Water represents knowledge and can assist with positive cash flow.

A window with a view of water can invite water energy into the home. You can also use a mirror to reflect the view of the water over a bed, desk and/or stove to bring more wealth into your life.

fire

THE ELEMENT OF FIRE IS RELATED TO THE COLOR RED AND THE FENG SHUI BAGUA AREA OF RECOGNITION. Fire also has the qualities of explosiveness, passion, and sincerity. The fire element creates earth, as ashes transform all back to the earth. Fire overcomes metal, as it causes metal to melt into a liquid.

You may have too much fire if you hold a lot of anger, blow up frequently, and stay angry for long periods of time. For this imbalance you can add earth, which depletes fire, or water, which puts out the flames. If you are fearful of anger and hold it all in, you may have too little fire. When you turn off fire, you also turn off the passion for life. For this imbalance you can add fire or wood, which feeds fire. When fire is balanced, you feel anger when appropriate, recognize and accept it, then let it go.

The red triangular shapes on the quilt are a fun way to add a little fire into your bedroom. Even the gray zigzags on the drapes add that triangular fire energy.

Fire is red and triangular in shape. In feng shui, fire elements improve passion and recognition. You can add fire to your home with the color red or even with lighting. Lighting and candles also represent fire energy. In some cases when you need to refresh your fire energy, it's a good idea to add a brighter, energy-efficient bulb to an existing light to reinvigorate that fire energy.

wood

THE ELEMENT OF WOOD IS RELATED TO THE COLORS GREEN AND BLUE AND THE FENG SHUI BAGUA AREAS OF NEW BEGINNINGS AND ABUNDANCE. Wood has the qualities of flexibility, life, and kindness. Wood also symbolizes growth. The wood element creates fire, like the logs in a fireplace. Wood overcomes earth, as the roots of a tree push through and take nourishment from the soil.

You may have too much wood if you are stubborn, inflexible, and unkind. For this imbalance you can add metal, which chops up wood, or fire, which burns up wood. If you are ungrounded, going this way and that way with the wind, such that you almost don't have a backbone, you may have too little wood. For this imbalance, you can add wood or water. When wood is balanced, you are well grounded and stable. You are flexible when you need to be but still hold steadfast to your ideals.

Wood objects to add to your space can be vertical or expansive, such as living plants. Green, living plants also improve the indoor air quality and add life energy to any space. Fake plants work similarly to living plants as long as they are of good quality and look real.

Green house plants by the window can bring in the wood element, but there are other ways too, such as the vertical lines of the blue drapes.

metal

THE ELEMENT OF METAL IS RELATED TO THE METALLIC COLORS, AS WELL AS WHITE AND GRAY, AND THE FENG SHUI BAGUA AREAS OF BENEFACTORS AND COMPLETION. Metal has the qualities of righteousness, contraction, and joy. The metal element creates water, as drops of water condense on a metal pipe. Metal overcomes wood, such as when an ax chops down a tree.

You may have too much metal if you are rigid and talk excessively without thinking. For this imbalance you can add water, which depletes metal, or fire, which melts and allows metals to be reshaped and refined. If you are unable to speak up for yourself when appropriate, you may have a metal deficiency. For this imbalance, you can add metal or earth, which produces metal. When metal is balanced, you speak and stand up for yourself and what is right appropriately and with thoughtful certainty.

Metal is associated with circular shapes and the physical element of metal. It assists in efficiency and attracting helpful people to your office. Ways to add the metal element to your space include using metal wind chimes or other natural metal objects. You can find metal Buddhas to balance the five elements in your space as well.

These simple and sturdy chairs are metal and silver in color, which are both qualities of the metal element. In addition, this beautiful metal leaf curtain can bring in this element with its metallic colors. When placed in a doorway, you can activate metal energy each time you walk through it.

BASIC FENG SHUI PRINCIPLES

POSITION YOURSELF IN COMMAND OF YOUR LIFE

THE POWER OF INTENTION

position yourself in command of your life

IN FENG SHUI WE HAVE A VERY IMPORTANT CONCEPT CALLED THE "COMMANDING POSITION." Ideally, your bed, desk, and stove are positioned so that you can see the door and the expanse of the room, and you have your back against the far wall. You don't want to be directly in front of the door. Instead, across the room, diagonal from the door, is typically the most ideal position.

Where does the idea of the commanding position come from? The feeling of danger and fear is a physiological response that you experience on a subtle level when you cannot see the door or what may be coming your way. Although not everyone is consciously aware of it, it does affect you. It is like water dripping lightly on a stone for years; the stress levels begin to wear you down. Metaphorically, the commanding position places you in command of the room, your home, and your life, because you can see what life brings to you, and you can move forward with your eyes open.

Understandably, this furniture placement may not always be possible, so you can make an adjustment to a potentially unfavorable position by placing a mirror in such a way that you can see the door to the room. Now you're back in command!

Locating your bed so that you can see the door but are not directly facing it places you in command of your life.

the power of intention

INTENTION IS AN IMPORTANT ASPECT IN FENG SHUI. Remember why you are doing whatever you do, whether you move your bed, add a crystal, or even utter a word. Each action sends vibrations into the universe and can affect you, your home, and even the universe as a whole.

Feng shui depends a lot upon your intention. If you add a green plant for more growth in a specific area of your life, the physical act of placing that object is just one part. The second part is to acknowledge that the placement of that object has created a shift in your energy to set the wheels in motion to achieve your goals.

Let the universe know through action and intention what you truly want, and I promise you will receive something remarkable in return.

Each feng shui adjustment is even more powerful when imbued with intention. When you select a Buddha, pick the one that you're drawn to. When you offer flowers, remember why. When you paint your wall pink, be sure you love it. When you sit in your chair, rest and take it all in.

SPACE CLEARING

tip 29

Objects absorb and record the qi of their owners. Take note of the energy of anything vintage or previously owned that you bring into your home. It may have some good qi, but it may also have energy you don't need or want.

re-dedicate your space

IN FENG SHUI, THERE IS A LOT OF TALK ABOUT "ENERGY" OR "QI." The qi of a space can influence the present and future circumstances of the inhabitants. Similarly, the "predecessor energy" of a home or object can greatly influence the current qi of a space. This applies to previous owners and residents, vintage furniture, and even used books. Does a place or object hold an imprint of positive, supportive energy? Or does it hold negative and stagnant qi?

Space clearing is an effective way to re-dedicate the invisible energy of a space. It is vital to clear the space of any stale energy and create a clean slate for you and your family. This is especially true if you have a lot of secondhand items.

Remember, once you clear the space or object of the negative energy, replace that energy with positive intention. The following tips offer different ways to clear space, including using orange peel and smudging.

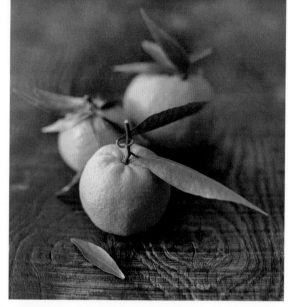

The scent of fresh orange peel can brighten any room.

refresh with orange peel

ON A TYPICAL DAY, I START WITH FIVE DROPS OF ORANGE AND ONE DROP OF FRANKINCENSE ESSENTIAL OILS IN MY DIFFUSER. This is my favorite way to clear my work space and begin to create.

In feng shui, oranges and orange peel represent vibrant, life-affirming yang energy. Yang energy is like the energy at high noon—bright and strong. Orange essence is refreshing and happy, and contributes positive, fresh, and brightening energy to our inner and outer environments. Orange essence will transform an area into a space with vibrant life, giving positive energy.

Fresh orange peel works best, but you can also use orange essential oil. Place the peel from one orange or 27 drops of the essential oil in a spray bottle and fill it with water. Walk around your home and spray this citrus essence all around, paying special attention to dead corners and closets. Orange peel carries vibrant life energy to clear, and in turn rejuvenate, you and your home. This is excellent to do on an annual or even monthly basis.

Just by opening all the windows and doors in your home, you will clear the space.

air it out!

A GREAT WAY TO CLEAR YOUR SPACE IS TO USE AN ORANGE-ESSENCE SPRAY IN CONJUNCTION WITH OPENING ALL OF THE WINDOWS AND EXTERIOR DOORS IN YOUR HOME. This is called "Changing the Qi of the Home."

First, open all of the windows and doors for a minimum of 15 minutes. Allow fresh air to move throughout the entire home. Second, purchase some orange essential spray or make your own with water and 27 drops of essential oil. Shake the bottle and spray nine times around each room in your home, starting at the entry door and moving around the perimeter of the room in a clockwise direction. When you end up back at the front door, set your intention to be that you are filling your home with bright white light and contentment.

It is good practice to clear your space at least once a year. The most auspicious time to do this is on Chinese New Year because the lunar new year is symbolically a great time to clear out the old, stale energy in your home to make space for new, positive energy.

Sage is one type of herb that can be used for smudging. You can also try sweet grass or palo santo, which is my personal favorite.

circumambulation and smudging

WHILE WE TRADITIONALLY USE ORANGE ESSENCE IN FENG SHUI FOR SPACE CLEARING, SMUDGING IS ANOTHER METHOD OF CLEARING A SPACE OF NEGATIVE QI. Smudging involves burning sacred herbs and using the smoke to shift energy. It is especially useful on an regular basis to refresh your home if you've had guests.

In general, the herb is ignited and then gently blown down to an ember to allow for spreading smoke around the room. It is important to guide the smoke to different areas of the room, including corners, inside closets, and in each direction of the compass. Also, be sure to allow the herb to produce enough smoke to fill the air.

The physical movement of walking around the perimeter of a space is described as circumambulating. Typically I recommend starting at the front door (or door to the room) and walking clockwise. Be present and remember to replace the cleared energy with positive intention.

smudging herbs

WHILE WHITE SAGE IS THE MOST COMMONLY
USED SUBSTANCE FOR SMUDGING, IT IS NOT THE
ONLY MATERIAL THAT CAN BE USED. Sage is easy
to find and is a good general space-clearing
material for releasing negative energy.

Native American traditions often include the
burning of sweet grass in their clearing rituals.
Sweet grass is said to be beneficial in attracting
positive spiritual energy and is especially
effective in combination with sage.

Tibetans burn juniper in ceremonies to
connect heaven, man, and earth. The smell
is very strong, and a little goes a long way.
Juniper is particularly useful for clearing
sacred objects.

Finally, my favorite method of space clearing
lately has been smudging with palo santo. As a
purifying agent, palo santo wood emits a better
smell than sage or juniper when burned. Palo
santo can be used as a matter of preference or
to avoid allergies. I love its fresh, bright, and
minty fragrance.

Regardless of which material you choose,
all of these options are time-tested and
ancient tools for clearing space and releasing
negative energy.

If you can't find herbs to burn, you can always
use incense instead.

tip 34

While you're at it, don't forget the floor vents and grilles. Clean all the parts of your HVAC regularly.

a literal space clearing

IF YOU LIVE IN A HOME WITH ANY SORT OF HVAC (HEATING, VENTILATION, AND AIR CONDITIONING) UNIT(S), YOU PROBABLY HAVE AN AIR FILTER SOMEWHERE. You might be surprised to find that this filter has a ton of dust and debris that needs some attention. This can literally affect your air quality!

Cleaning HVAC filters and coils helps your appliances run more efficiently because the accumulated debris restricts airflow. When filters and coils are clean, the units use less energy, which saves you money. Some filters can be cleaned and reused, while others may need to be replaced.

In addition, cleaning filters regularly improves the indoor air quality. Filters may harbor bacteria, mold, or allergens. Regularly cleaning filters will minimize any indoor-air-quality issues.

make your heart sing

WHAT MAKES YOUR HEART SING? Did you know that the Recognition area of the feng shui bagua map also governs passion, fire, and the heart? When we sing, we activate fire energy within our hearts. In addition, the area of Completion is related to the mouth and joyfulness.

Take some time every day to sing! Singing not only exercises your lungs and abdominal muscles, it releases endorphins for positive energy. If you're a little shy about it, sing when no one is around. Just sing for yourself. Who cares if your pitch isn't perfect?!

When I sing, I visualize the sound waves twirling through the air toward the other end of the room. This fills the entire room with positive energy and joy. It does not hurt to dance around as well!

Creating a space to listen to music in the home reminds us to invite singing and joy into our lives. Don't let those records collect dust!

ENTRY

MAKE AN INVITING ENTRY

BRIGHTEN YOUR ENTRY

CLEAN YOUR ENTRY

REFRESH YOUR FRONT DOOR

START USING YOUR FRONT DOOR

ADD A FOUNTAIN

tip 36

make an inviting entry

IT IS IMPORTANT TO KEEP YOUR DOOR AND
ENTRANCE TIDY, BUT THIS AREA SHOULD ALSO
BE INVITING AND EASY TO FIND.

In feng shui, your entry symbolizes
opportunities to find you. How will an amazing
person or project find you if your door cannot
be found? Is it hidden behind bushes or clutter?
Is the doorbell broken? Make sure your door is
easy to find by painting it red, or even adding
plants around the door. Trim overgrown bushes
or remove clutter that may be blocking the
visibility of your door, and fix the doorbell
and buzzer!

Other areas to check include the door
number and mat. Is your door number easy
to find? Is it clean and secured to the exterior
of your home? Is there a clean doormat?
Greeting guests with a new doormat invites
positive energy.

Remember, not only is your entry the first
thing that people see when they visit your
home, it is also the first thing that you see when
you get home. Make sure it is visible and clean!

Opportunities have the best chance of finding you
if you have an inviting entry like this one, with
a red door, beautiful flowers, and an easily seen
house number.

You can brighten your entry energetically. It's fine to have useful things in your entry, like your hat and shoes. Your loved and cared for everyday belongings infuse the entry of your home with your illuminating life energy.

brighten your entry

THE FIRST THING PEOPLE SEE WHEN THEY VISIT YOUR HOME IS THE ENTRY. What is it that they see? Is the entry well-lit? Is it welcoming? Can visitors find the front door easily? The entry and front door of your home represent your face to the world, how the world sees you, and how easily opportunities can come to you.

One way to brighten your entry is literally. Make sure you have a bright and energy-saving light bulb illuminating the entry.

Another option is to hang a feng shui, faceted crystal ball in a dark or small entry. The crystal attracts positive energy, and then disperses it into your home.

In feng shui it is very important to hang crystal balls using a red cord. Red is a very auspicious color and represents protection. It is even better if the cord can be a length that equals a multiple of 9—like 9, 18, or 27 inches. Feng shui crystals are easy to find online, and they come in various sizes. For feng shui purposes, most interior spaces should use crystals of ¼in (40mm) in diameter or larger.

A clean entry doesn't have to be completely empty. A well-placed coat rack not only offers a place to rest your necessary hat and scarf, but it adds life energy to your entry.

clean your entry

THE ENTRY AREA OF YOUR HOME, INCLUDING THE EXTERIOR AND INTERIOR, REPRESENTS THE "MOUTH OF QI"—WHERE ENERGY COMES INTO YOUR HOME. If this area is congested, cluttered, and in disarray, how can positive energy flow into your life with ease?

Start cleaning the entry areas of your home. Vacuum your welcome mat, toss all the clutter that has accumulated over time, and sweep up the dusty corners. It is important to clean out this area and keep it clean and fresh so you can attract the best energy in your life.

The door to your living space is something you see every day as you come home, and it affects you and your mood. A clean and cared-for entry will give your home and your visitors a sense of place and stability.

refresh your front door

WALK OUTSIDE TO YOUR FRONT DOOR, AND TAKE A GOOD
LOOK AT WHAT YOU SEE. I'm talking about the actual formal
entry door to your home.

Make sure to clean your front door of any dirt and dust.
Clean around and inside the door jamb and frame, as well
as the edges of the door, where dust collects. These areas
are often overlooked. Repaint or clean your entry door and
make sure that the doorbell, buzzer, and all door hardware
are in working condition. Oil any squeaky hinges, and clean
or replace the number and name on the door.

Take care to sweep under and vacuum the welcome mat.
Because the entry door is your mouth of qi, this is where
energy can enter your home. An excellent way to attract
more qi is to get a new doormat. Get a new welcome mat,
red or black if possible, to attract qi. Ideally, you want to get
one that is almost the same width as your front door, or a
little larger, not too small. When your entry door stands out,
you can differentiate yourself and attract auspicious energy
into your home and life.

The doorknob is touched several
times a day and can easily collect
dirt. Be sure to pay attention to
the details. Your doorknob works
hard for you, thank it and give it
a little TLC.

Remember to use the "official" front door to your home whenever you can to maximize the potential for attracting positive energy into your home and life.

start using your front door

AS MANY OF US ARE CAR-DEPENDENT, WE OFTEN USE THE GARAGE OR SIDE DOOR AS THE PRIMARY ENTRANCE. It's more convenient and requires less walking.

In feng shui, your formal front door represents the mouth of qi as well as your face to the world. This is how energy, good luck, and opportunities come to you. So if you're not using your front door regularly, that energy has no way of getting into your home and life! Worse, if you keep this important portal closed all the time, you are not able to maximize your opportunities, and you close yourself off from receiving positive energy.

The best way to remedy this situation is simple. Start using your front door again. If possible, open it every day, or at the very least nine times a month. Make an effort to walk around to the front and encourage the beneficial energy to flow and enter your home. If you forget about using it, you miss opportunities to bring positive energy into your life and home.

add a fountain

A WATER FOUNTAIN IS ONE OF THOSE
QUINTESSENTIAL FENG SHUI CURES THAT
EVERYONE ASKS ABOUT. Not only does it
provide a soothing sound, the moving water
can improve your cash flow.

A good location for a fountain would be
in the entry of your home, but it is important
that the flow of the water is toward your home.
For this reason, fountains with a directional
water flow are best. It is helpful to have a
fountain that you really love and care for. It
is also helpful to have all five elements
represented in some way.

Water fountains are great ways to add beauty,
sound, and humidity for a tranquil and
harmonious space. The soothing sounds of
trickling water can relax your mind and lower
your stress level. The circulating water also
releases negative ions, which helps to purify
the air. Just like waterfalls and the ocean, the
negative ions produced by the circulating water
improve mood and induce feelings of well-
being. The water also creates humidity that
moistens the air for humans and for plants.
A fountain is a natural humidifier!

When selecting a water fountain for a feng shui
adjustment, first pick one that you love. And second,
if possible, choose a fountain where the water flows
in one general direction like this one. Even with an
outdoor fountain, the flow of the water can be
directed toward the center of your home so the good
qi comes to you, rather than flows away from you.

LIVING ROOM

A SPACE TO LIVE AND ENTERTAIN

FISH TANKS

NINE FRESH ORANGES

a space to live and entertain

THE LIVING ROOM IS A SPACE TO GATHER, LIVE, AND
ENTERTAIN. IN FENG SHUI, THIS ROOM IS BEST LOCATED
NEAR THE FRONT OF THE HOME. After the foyer, the living
room is the most ideal room to encounter as you enter
your home. This living room position allows an individual
to immediately decompress and relax into the space.

Spend some time arranging your furniture so that most
of it is in the commanding position. For instance, it is
welcoming and pleasant to face the front of the sofa
when you walk in rather than see the back of it.

With the trend in open-plan homes, it is great to have
the spaciousness and integration of eating and cooking, but
I find that we still seek intimate areas within the openness.
Therefore, take some time to make a variety of spaces in
your living room that support different experiences, such
as a pair of matching chairs to encourage a one-on-one
conversation, or a quiet window seat for reading.

A living room can invite you
to rest and enjoy time with
loved ones. The layout of your
furniture can encourage
conversation and interaction.

fish tanks

IN ASIAN MYTHOLOGY, THERE IS A STORY OF A
GOLDFISH OR CARP THAT TRANSFORMED INTO
A DRAGON. Dragons represent luck and power.
In turn, goldfish are auspicious. They can be
brought into your home to attract success.
For a wealth cure, try adopting eight orange
goldfish and one black goldfish.

The ideal location of your tank really depends
on your floor plan, but as a general rule, for
wealth it may be beneficial to place the fish
near the front door of your home, especially
in the Path in Life (KAN) area of the feng shui
bagua map.

If there is a water filter on your tank with any
sort of waterfall, it is best to position it so the
water falls toward the central part of your home.
This represents the cash flowing toward you.
You can also place a fish tank in the Abundance
(XUN) area of your living room. My teacher,
Steven Post, suggests locating the tank at eye
level, so it is easily accessible to view and touch
and creates a sense of peace.

An aquarium creates constant
motion in your home,
representing energy and change.
Be sure to take good care and
accommodate your fish with the
largest tank possible so they have
a happy life (which can contribute
to better qi for you).

nine fresh oranges

IN FENG SHUI, ORANGES AND ORANGE PEELS
CONTRIBUTE POSITIVE, FRESH, AND BRIGHTENING
ENERGY TO OUR INNER AND OUTER
ENVIRONMENTS. Oranges are very auspicious
and lucky in Chinese culture. You can always
find oranges as decorations at any Chinese
festivity. Oranges can transform the home
with vibrant life, giving positive energy.

An easy way to incorporate oranges as a
home decoration is to get a lovely bowl.
A green, black, or white bowl complements
the color orange well. Place this bowl in your
living room, taking care to keep the fruit fresh
and replenished as the oranges start to get
too ripe. When they get very ripe, feel free to
eat them!

A group of nine oranges in your favorite bowl is a
wonderful way to bring auspicious qi into your living
room. A green bowl adds life, a black bowl wisdom,
or a white bowl clarity.

KITCHEN

A PLACE TO NOURISH

DEEP CLEAN THE REFRIGERATOR

SWITCH TO NON-TOXIC CLEANING PRODUCTS

START COMPOSTING

SWITCH TO FABRIC TOWELS AND NAPKINS

USE YOUR DISHWASHER

DOUBLE YOUR BURNERS

CAN YOU SEE YOUR STOVE
FROM THE FRONT DOOR?

REDUCE BOTTLED WATER USAGE

ROTATE THE USE OF YOUR STOVE BURNERS

GO GREEN ON TAKEOUT

CLEARLY MARK YOUR RECYCLING BINS

a place to nourish

THE KITCHEN IS THE ROOM IN WHICH WE STORE AND COOK THE FOOD THAT NOURISHES US. I like to think of it as a modern hearth, a place where families gather for warmth around the fire. This is especially the case with today's open-plan kitchens.

In feng shui it is said that white is the best color for a kitchen, because it represents cleanliness. Similarly to how white is the ideal color for plates to show off the rainbow of colors in foods, white is also a great color for the walls, cabinets, and backsplash tile of a kitchen.

In particular with kitchen cabinets, be aware of upper cabinets and shelves that do not go all the way to the ceiling. The open space between the top of the cabinets and the ceiling is a place where blocked energy can collect, leading to arguments. If this is something you cannot change, you can put plants, lighting, or beautiful objects in this space to keep the energy alive.

This is a skillful example of placing beautiful and loved objects on top of upper cabinets to keep the energy alive in the kitchen. Be sure to keep this area clean and free of dust.

deep clean the refrigerator

THE REFRIGERATOR IS AN IMPORTANT APPLIANCE IN YOUR HOME, AND IT REPRESENTS BOUNDARIES IN LIFE AND HOW YOU NOURISH YOURSELF IN THE WORLD. It's a good idea to have a well-stocked refrigerator—not too full and not too empty. Or, as we say in feng shui, not too yin and not too yang.

Look at this as an opportunity to deep clean and de-clutter. Empty out your refrigerator and remove anything expired, old, and/or spoiled. Spoiled and expired food symbolizes neglect of one's overall health. If possible, compost the organic material, or find a compost drop-off location, and recycle or reuse the glass and plastic containers.

When cleaning the interior of the refrigerator, I prefer to use natural, non-toxic cleaners such as baking soda to scrub and a mixture of vinegar, water, and eucalyptus essential oil to wipe down and disinfect. Open up a new container of baking soda to absorb any odors in your newly organized and clean refrigerator.

I also keep a clear natural crystal quartz in my refrigerator. I program that crystal with the intention to enhance the life energy and nourishment of the food that I will later eat.

Don't forget to de-clutter your refrigerator on occasion. Keep healthy and fresh food in your home.

tip 47

The kitchen is where we prepare meals to nourish our bodies so it's really important to use healthy and non-toxic cleaning products in this area.

switch to non-toxic cleaning products

THE INDOOR AIR QUALITY OF OUR HOMES IS OFTEN OVERLOOKED BUT IS ESSENTIAL FOR HEALTH AND HEALING. Americans spend over 90 percent of our time indoors! It is time to eliminate toxic chemicals from your living environment. These chemicals are absorbed easily through the air and skin, and are extremely dangerous if swallowed.

Non-toxic, green cleaning products are now easy to find at your local grocery stores. It is also easy to make your own with household items like vinegar and baking soda.

My favorite DIY recipe is for an all-purpose cleaning solution. You combine one part white vinegar and three parts water, with nine drops of essential oil. Eucalyptus and tea tree oil are good options, as they are naturally anti-bacterial and anti-microbial. Shake up all of the ingredients in a spray bottle and you've got a homemade, non-toxic cleaner.

start composting

THE BENEFITS OF COMPOSTING ARE NUMEROUS, WHETHER OR NOT YOU GARDEN OR HAVE A YARD. Composting drastically reduces organic waste from kitchen scraps and organic yard waste, so you save money on your waste bill while reducing greenhouse-gas emissions through proper degradation. Plus, composting recycles nutrition for the soil.

When you compost organic materials, instead of dooming them into landfill, you prevent production of harmful gases like methane and leachate formulation.

If you live in an apartment without outdoor space to compost, search for local compost drop-off sites.

Composting is among the top options for reducing your carbon footprint, thus doing your part to save our planet. From enriching soil without harmful chemicals to reducing a trash collection bill, time spent composting is time well spent.

How wonderful it is to take organic waste and use it to nourish the plants in your home, such as a herb garden on your kitchen windowsill. Compost can add life energy to the food you eat.

Fabric towels and napkins can be beautiful kitchen accessories for your kitchen. Your choice of pattern or color is an elegant way to bring in feng shui elements. Or you can just pick what you like to make the space fun and personalize it with your unique qi.

switch to fabric towels and napkins

ACCORDING TO THE NATURAL RESOURCES DEFENSE COUNCIL, "IF EVERY HOUSEHOLD IN THE UNITED STATES REPLACED JUST ONE ROLL OF VIRGIN FIBER PAPER TOWELS (70 SHEETS) WITH 100% RECYCLED ONES, WE COULD SAVE 544,000 TREES."

You can save both money and trees by using reusable and washable fabric items in place of disposable paper towels and napkins. Microfiber towels are especially good substitutes for paper towels for cleaning glass, electronics, and stainless steel surfaces. Microfiber is super absorbent, lint-free, and leaves no streaks. As for napkins, fabric napkins are much more sophisticated and useful than any paper napkins. I have a set of fancy ones for dinner parties and guests, as well as a stack of nice kitchen tea towels that I use as my "everyday" napkins.

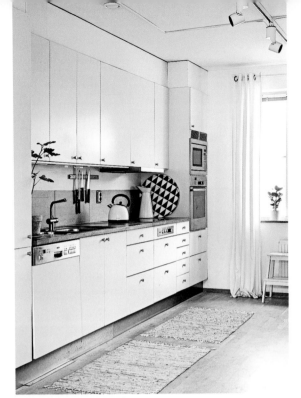

Using a dishwasher saves water and can sterilize your dishes. This kitchen also illustrates an idea of what to do if your cabinets don't reach the ceiling: you can build a soffit down to close the space where stagnant qi can collect.

use your dishwasher

EVERYONE LIKES THIS ONE! One great way to preserve water in your home is to use your dishwasher. Most dishwashers now use less water than washing by hand.

Typical dishwashers use approximately 15 gallons (56 liters) of water per load. The newer ones use even less. This equals less than five seconds to wash and dry each dish, and I know it takes longer than five minutes to handwash a load of dishes. Save the most water by running full loads only.

Be sure to use phosphate-free dishwasher detergent, and turn off the heated dry, if possible, for energy savings and extra green points.

If you don't have a dishwasher, soak your dishes, rather than running the water while washing, to save tremendous amounts of water.

Ideally your stove should be in the commanding position of the kitchen. If you are not in command at the stove, a mirrored object (similar to this pot) can cleverly substitute as a mirror so you can see behind you (and put yourself back in the commanding position). Just be sure you can clearly see the door behind you and keep the mirrored object clean and very reflective.

double your burners

YOUR STOVE REPRESENTS YOUR WEALTH AND HOW YOU NOURISH YOURSELF IN THE WORLD. If you are not able to eat well, how can you perform your best?

Make sure your stove is in the commanding position. This means that you can see the main entry of your kitchen while using the stove. If this is not possible, set up a mirror behind or next to the stove so you can see the door.

Not only will a mirror bring your stove into command, but it can also multiply your burners. In feng shui, the more burners you have, the more possibility for wealth. It's like more irons in the fire! Even if your stove is in command, you can still set up a mirror that reflects your burners. The more burners, the more abundance and prosperity for the inhabitants of the home.

can you see your stove from the front door?

GO TO THE FRONT DOOR OF YOUR HOME. Can you see your stove? In feng shui this is a very dangerous set up, and can contribute to conflict in the home.

Because this may be a difficult layout to change without doing renovations, a remedial solution is to put up a wall or some kind of visual separation so the sight line from the front door to the stove is blocked. I have used norens (traditional Japanese fabric dividers) in kitchen doorways to adjust this sort of feng shui no-no. Just remember to block the view of the burner!

If that's not possible, as a last resort you can put a feng shui crystal ball up between the door and the stove to counteract the negative qi.

One option is to use a frosted glass or acrylic panel to obscure the view of the stove from the front door.

It's very easy to add a water filter tap to your existing kitchen sink. Healthy water and reduced plastics, it's a win-win!

reduce bottled water usage

CONTRARY TO POPULAR BELIEF, BOTTLED WATER IS "SUBJECT TO LESS RIGOROUS TESTING AND PURITY STANDARDS THAN THOSE WHICH APPLY TO CITY TAP WATER," SAYS THE NATURAL RESOURCES DEFENSE COUNCIL (NRDC). Health-wise, plastics are terrible to drink from. There may be Bisphenol A (BPA) or other toxic chemicals and substances in plastic containers that will affect water quality.

Plastic water bottles are also unhealthy for our environment. They take thousands of years to biodegrade and usually end up in landfills.

Water filters are a good way to reduce your environmental footprint while taking care of your health. They can remove contaminants such as rust, dirt, chlorine, lead, silt, and odors, and help you reduce usage of plastic water bottles.

I use a high-quality water filter and drink tap water whenever possible. I also use reusable glass bottles and a seltzer machine as much as possible at home.

The everyday ritual of lighting your stove supports your prosperity in the world. Let it be a reminder to nourish and love yourself.

rotate the use of your stove burners

MY FAVORITE BURNER ON MY STOVE IS THE ONE ON THE FRONT RIGHT. Which one is your favorite? In feng shui, your stove represents nourishment, as well as career, fame, and wealth. The stove is a modern hearth, the place in the home that provides warmth, safety, and nourishment. This means it is essential to use your stove every day, even if only to boil water, and to keep it very clean and in working order. All of the burners should work properly, and you should wipe down the stove on a daily basis.

So what does this have to do with your favorite burner? Tomorrow when you go to your stove, try using another burner instead of always going to the same one. Open up some opportunities for yourself for success in career, fame, and wealth. Instead of mindlessly using the same "favorite" burner, intentionally make an effort toward something new every day. Again, use the stove at least once every day.

go green on takeout

WHEN WE EAT PREPARED FOOD, NOT ONLY ARE THERE TAKEOUT CONTAINERS, THERE ARE STACKS OF PAPER NAPKINS AS WELL AS PLASTICWARE THAT YOU USUALLY DO NOT NEED.

The US population tosses out enough paper and plastic cups, forks, and spoons every year to circle the equator 300 times. Help save millions of tons of paper and plastic each year by simply asking the restaurant to not include paper napkins and plasticware. In many online ordering systems, there is even a checkbox for eco-friendly ordering!

Even when eating takeout, the details matter. Practically, we can reduce waste by requesting no napkins and plasticware (even saying no to compostable plastics). Energetically, we can plate our food and sit down for a meal. Every event can become a sacred, meaningful ritual to enrich and bring joy to our lives.

It's helpful to create a place to locate the recycling bins, such as in the pantry or under the sink. If you keep the bins on the smaller side, you'll empty them more often!

clearly mark your recycling bins

IT IS COMMON KNOWLEDGE THAT RECYCLING HELPS THE ENVIRONMENT BY DIVERTING WASTE FROM LANDFILLS. Although you may know what type of material goes in each bin, it doesn't mean that the other members of your household (or guests) are familiar with the setup.

It only takes a few moments to clearly mark your recycling bins. First, take note of the separation requirements of your municipal recycling. For instance, I have one bin for paper and another for glass, metals, and rigid plastics, because they need to be separated to be recycled by my city's service. Sometimes you can ruin a whole bag of paper by accidentally tossing food into a recycling bin.

DINING ROOM

ALL ABOUT THE DINING ROOM

USE YOUR DINING TABLE

FRESH FLOWERS FOR JOY

tip 57

A great example of a dining table with welcoming rounded corners and cheerful lighting.

all about the dining room

IN GENERAL, THE DINING ROOM IS A PLACE WHERE OUR FAMILIES GATHER NOT ONLY TO NOURISH OUR BODIES BUT ALSO TO CONNECT WITH EACH OTHER.

The best dining tables have rounded corners, such as oval or circular tables. A round table symbolizes equality and balance. Rectangular and square tables are okay as long as the corners are not too sharp. Make sure that there are enough chairs for each person in the household. This allows every inhabitant to feel acknowledged and nurtured.

Finally, be sure the room is well lit and cared for. If possible, there should be no televisions (which encourage mindless eating), and the décor should feature yang colors that help digestion. Light and bright colors such as blue, green, red, and pink are appetizing and encourage a positive dining experience.

use your dining table

SADLY, NOWADAYS DINING TABLES TEND TO BE
USED FOR EVERYTHING BUT DINING. If possible,
take some time each day to eat mindfully at
your dining table.

The dining table symbolizes a space to
nourish and feed the body, especially with
family and friends. Using it on a daily basis
prevents it from collecting dust and clutter
and allows you to take some time to
nurture yourself.

Since space is often at a minimum, a dining
table often doubles as a daytime desk, or you
might not have a dining table at all. If you use
your dining table as a desk, be sure to put
away your work while you eat. If you don't have
a dining table, create a small space somewhere
that is dedicated to eating one meal. Perhaps
clear off the coffee table, keep the TV off, and
find a beautiful placemat and dish to serve
yourself your meal of choice.

You can make every meal mindful
by creating a space for it. A lovely
placemat, a glass of water, and
plating your food can all help to
make even dinner for one a
nourishing experience.

fresh flowers for joy

FRESH FLOWERS CAN BRING IN JOY AND UPLIFT THE QI OF YOUR HOME. I find them particularly amazing when located in the dining room, right on the dining table.

It is always great to bring in local and seasonal flowers if possible. Conventional flowers are factory-grown and flown in refrigerated planes from halfway around the world, which is not exactly environmentally friendly. Often they are sprayed with toxic chemicals and preservatives to make them last longer. It's also great to support local farmers.

Be sure to keep flowers refreshed by replacing the water on a daily basis and removing any dead leaves and flowers.

Flowers bring joy and celebrate life energy in a home. They can always lift the qi of a space, especially in the dining room. Select the flowers that you're drawn to, and if you're curious, you can look up the symbolism of the blooms that you are most attracted to.

HOME OFFICE

CREATE A SEPARATE SPACE

PUT YOUR DESK IN COMMAND

LOOK AT THE CLUTTER ON YOUR DESK

GO PAPERLESS!

AVOID GLASS DESKTOPS

BUY POST-CONSUMER-RECYCLED PRODUCTS

WHAT ARE YOU FACING AT YOUR DESK?

BRING CLARITY AND FOCUS TO YOUR WORK

PLANT IN PROSPERITY CORNER

create a separate space

It's essential to separate the home office when you are seeking a better work-life balance. One option is to use a plant as a screen. A green plant also brings in more life energy for growth in your career. This desk is facing a door (on the left), so it's in command (see tip 61, page 104), but you could use a mirror to expand your view (see tip 66, page 110).

YOUR HOME OFFICE REPRESENTS AN IMPORTANT AREA IN YOUR HOME. In feng shui, this area symbolizes your career, wealth, and how you bring yourself wealth in the world. A few simple changes in your home office will support your career and wealth.

If you are able to, dedicate an entire room to your home office. This is the ideal scenario.

If you do not have enough rooms to dedicate one for your office, do your best to separate your desk within the space it is in. You can do this with a freestanding bookcase or a room divider, or even with a fabric panel or drape. This is especially important in a bedroom or living room, to help you focus while working and disengage when not working. Visual boundaries are very important in keeping your work and play times balanced. At the very least, you can get a beautiful piece of fabric or scarf and cover your desk when office hours are over!

The most important feng shui principle to review for your career is the location of your desk. If you can be in command while working, you can invite the most opportunities and maximize your potential.

put your desk in command

TAKE A LOOK AT YOUR DESK LOCATION IN RELATION TO THE ROOM'S DOOR. I often see clients with their desks facing the wall, leaving their backs to the door. This is a major feng shui no-no. Ideally, you should position your desk so that you can see the door while not being directly in line with the door.

The most auspicious position for your desk is at a diagonal from the door. The desired orientation, called the commanding position, is when you are facing the door and the expanse of the room. This means that you are in command of your life and your career, and can see what the universe has in store for you. The best opportunities will be available to you, and you will be able to see them coming. This position minimizes stress and allows the best flow of energy while working.

If space is at a premium in your home and you cannot face the door, set up a mirror so that while you are sitting at your desk you can easily see the door in the reflection. Small, concave mirrors found in automobile shops are excellent for this job. And remember to keep a minimum of 36 inches (90 cm) clear behind the desk for your chair. This represents the space for your business to grow.

It's illuminating to see where you tend to clutter your desk, but sometimes the stacks of paper need to happen, and it's ok. Just be mindful to address the clutter and take care of it in a timely manner. I clear my desk every morning; it's like clearing my head to start the day afresh.

look at the clutter on your desk

TAKE A LOOK AT YOUR DESK CLUTTER TO FOCUS ON ANY PROBLEM AREAS THAT MIGHT BE AFFECTING YOUR CAREER AND WEALTH.

Where does your clutter tend to accumulate on your desk? While sitting at your desk, look at the furthest left corner, the furthest middle/top area, and the furthest right corner of your desk. Is there a place that you always pile up paperwork that you plan to get to "one day"? Is there a stack of magazines you're hoping to go through? Is there a specific area you stash all of the mail you haven't opened yet? Clutter on the top left corner may represent stagnation in your cash flow and money. The middle top symbolizes how people are viewing you, which is your fame and reputation. Maybe you need more visibility and/or recognition. The furthest right corner is the relationship area. This may indicate the need to cultivate new and existing relationships.

What is the clutter, and what does it symbolize to you based on the area of your desk it's in?

go paperless!

WE RECEIVE PILES OF JUNK SNAIL MAIL EVERY DAY—CREDIT-CARD APPLICATIONS, CATALOGS, BILLS—AND TYPICALLY IT GOES STRAIGHT INTO THE TRASH. Going paperless is a simple, pain-free way to stop these mailbox fillers in their tracks and reduce the amount of wasted paper our society creates daily.

First, please recycle whatever junk mail you receive. It is a good idea to shred anything with your name on it, and then recycle the paper material. Check your local recycling guidelines to see just how much of this mail—catalogs, magazines, etc.—is eligible for recycling, and put as much of it as possible through the earth-saving cycle!

Second, take a few minutes to unsubscribe to catalogs and switch to paperless billing. You not only save trees, you help save energy, carbon emissions, paper waste, and water.

Third, thank yourself for reducing the vast amount of annoying ads and attempts to increase your monthly spending that come to your home regularly. And know that you've taken a huge step toward preserving the only earth we have.

Magazines, periodicals, and catalogs can pile up! Here's a fun way to reuse the paper: as a side table on wheels. You can also use magazine images for vision boards. But, it's usually best to cancel and recycle anything unsolicited and unnecessary.

A solid wooden desk stabilizes and provides grounding to your work in the world.

avoid glass desktops

YOUR DESK POSITION IS IMPORTANT IN FENG SHUI AS IT REPRESENTS YOUR CAREER AND PATH IN LIFE. You should also look at what material your desk is made of.

Although glass desktops are attractive, modern, and sleek, in feng shui terms they are not ideal if you want success in your career. The transparency of the top may cause important deals and projects to fall through. The delicate nature of glass also makes it difficult to really pore over your work.

Feng shui recommends getting an opaque, solid desktop to ensure financial stability and success in your work. A brown wooden desk can represent earthy stability in your career. A metal desk may assist those in need of additional focus and help improve precision in your work.

buy post-consumer-recycled products

MOST OF US KNOW BY NOW THAT WE NEED TO RECYCLE. We have heard it many times: reduce, reuse, and recycle! Note that "recycle" is last on that list. Post-consumer-recycled content is made at least partially from materials that people put in public or private recycling bins. So this material has gone through the hands of a consumer. A label that simply says "recycled" indicates that the product was likely made from virgin material such as leftover scraps from factories or overproduced items.

Why buy post-consumer-recycled products? The items you recycle through municipal recycling eventually need to be purchased by someone in order to be fully recycled. When people like us purchase post-consumer-recycled products, we create a market demand for post-consumer materials. Sadly, if there's no market for those materials, everything we recycle may just end up in a landfill. For the sake of the environment, a good percentage of the paper and plastics that already exist should be salvaged and reused for post-consumer-recycled products.

Please choose post-consumer-recycled paper and other office supplies whenever possible. By creating a market and demand for these products, we can support and grow the infrastructure for green living.

There are so many options for post-consumer-recycled products: paper, plastic, and so forth. It takes a bit more effort, but it makes a difference! I encourage you to take a little extra time and spend your money on products that support rather than deplete the environment.

what are you facing at your desk?

A couple of ideas if you have your desk facing the wall: create a vision board, or add images and artworks that are inspiring and expansive.

WHAT ARE YOU FACING WHEN YOU ARE SITTING AT YOUR DESK? In the feng shui world, we encourage you to face into the room, in "command" of your life and career.

If this is not possible, and you must face a wall, there are a few ways to improve this situation. You can put a mirror on the wall in front of your desk. Rather than looking at a wall, which represents a block in your forward movement, the mirror will expand your view and allow you to move ahead in your career.

Often people will orient their desks toward a window and an outdoor view. In my experience, although it's nice to face a view, it's not the best position for someone who wants to advance his or her career. Your energy goes out the window and does not stay with your work. Instead, why not have the window to your side so that you can take in the view when you want a break, but it's not distracting you from achieving your career and wealth goals?

A mirror in front of your desk can expand your view, opportunities, and wisdom. Just be sure that it's hung at eye level.

bring clarity and focus to your work

MIRRORS ARE USED FREQUENTLY AS FENG SHUI ADJUSTMENT OBJECTS. They can expand your view, eliminate bad energy, and add positive energy. In your home office, you can use a mirror to bring clarity and focus to your work.

Place a small (about a 3 inch/7.5 cm diameter), round mirror on the ceiling such that it reflects down on you. It's best to situate this mirror so that it is right above your head while you are sitting at your desk. Be sure it is securely fastened to the ceiling so you feel safe.

The mirror can elevate your qi, providing support for your mental focus and clarity in all aspects of your career and work life, which will in turn provide abundance and support.

plant in prosperity corner

The Abundance area of your desk is the top left corner, and while a green plant is most ideal, fresh branches and/or flowers can also do the trick. Change the water frequently and be sure to replace flowers when they start to wilt.

ASIDE FROM PUTTING YOUR DESK IN A COMMANDING POSITION, ANOTHER POWERFUL WAY TO ATTRACT ABUNDANCE IN YOUR CAREER AND WORK IS TO ACTIVATE THE ABUNDANCE AREA OF YOUR HOME OFFICE.

Stand in the doorway facing into the room or area that is your home office. The area to the far left back is the Prosperity corner of your office. Alternatively, you can locate the Abundance corner of your desktop. While sitting at your desk, the far left corner of the desktop is the Abundance area. You can stimulate prosperity by purchasing a new, green plant and placing it in this area. In fact, you can even place a plant in both locations for some extra support.

Plants represent growth and flexibility. They attract life and positivity. If you like lucky bamboo, place three stalks in a vase to represent growth in your abundance and wealth.

BATHROOM

Modern spa-like bathrooms now represent rest and relaxation, but it's still a good idea to keep the door closed as much as possible.

bathroom basics

IN TRADITIONAL FENG SHUI, THE BATHROOM IS A PLACE WHERE WATER IS ALWAYS COMING IN AND OUT OF THE HOME. Because water represents wealth and money flow, the bathroom is often seen as a problematic room.

My teachers have taught me one disclaimer: at the time that feng shui was developed, bathrooms in ancient China were very different to how they are today in the West. We see them as a luxurious, spa-like place of relaxation. So, although it is important to look at the bathroom, keep in mind cultural differences.

In general, take care to keep your toilet seat closed, as well as the bathroom door. This will keep the wealth from flowing away from you. On a practical note, the water in the toilet bowl contributes to the humidity in the room. Mold and mildew come from humidity and moisture! By keeping your toilet seat closed, you reduce the humidity in the air, thereby creating a cleaner and healthier environment.

turn off the water when brushing your teeth

WATER IS A PRECIOUS COMMODITY, AND WE NEED TO CONSERVE IT. We use up clean water faster than the earth can naturally recycle and purify it. Water conservation is essential to living a healthy, holistic lifestyle.

An easy way to preserve water in your home is to turn off the tap when brushing your teeth. I know this seems like a no-brainer, but not a lot of people do this. Simply turn on the water when you need it rather than letting it run while you are actively brushing your teeth. There is absolutely no reason to have water running straight down the drain.

Remember, leaving the water on for even a minute can mean one or more gallons of clean water down the drain!

Clean water is truly precious. Our bodies are over 60% water and we need clean water to live. It's a shame to waste our natural resources, so make sure every drop counts.

tip 71

While modern plumbing fixtures use less water, older and vintage models may unnecessarily waste water. Installing an aerator is a simple way to save some water in your everyday life.

water-saving aerator

CONSIDER GETTING A LOW-FLOW AERATOR FOR YOUR BATHROOM FAUCET. Low-flow aerators reduce the amount of water coming out of your faucets, but do not reduce the water pressure. Depending on the type of faucet, these can be found at your local hardware store for very little money.

Average faucets have a water flow of 3 gallons per minute (GPM). You can check on the side of your faucet to confirm; sometimes the GPM is stamped on the metal.

An aerator restricts the amount of water that goes through the faucet and also mixes in tiny bubbles of air (hence, "aerate"), so you won't notice a difference in water pressure. This device simply screws on to the mouth of your faucet for easy installation.

Generally, an aerator that limits the water flow to 2.2 GPM or less is considered low-flow. Aerators advertise their GPM on their sides.

So if you have a 3 GPM faucet, you could reduce your water usage by half simply by installing a 1.5 GPM aerator.

Reducing paper products in general is a wonderful way to conserve resources.

post-consumer-recycled toilet paper

ACCORDING TO THE NATURAL RESOURCES DEFENSE COUNCIL, "IF EVERY HOUSEHOLD IN THE UNITED STATES REPLACED JUST ONE ROLL OF VIRGIN FIBER TOILET PAPER WITH 100% RECYCLED ONES, WE COULD SAVE 423,900 TREES."

So, what can we do? Purchase post-consumer-recycled toilet paper! "Recycled" typically means that the content is made from pre-consumer materials, such as the leftover waste from manufacturing. It's good, but not the same as post-consumer. "Post-consumer recycled" indicates that the recycled portion of the product is from consumer waste, like pizza boxes or other materials that people have bought, used, and then separated for recycling. By purchasing post-consumer content, you divert waste from choking our landfills. Recycling truly makes a difference when consumers purchase products manufactured from recycled content.

If we make an effort to purchase more post-consumer-recycled toilet paper, we in turn create a demand for the recycled paper, which will minimize deforestation for virgin paper materials. Plus, they make soft versions now!

make your own low-flow toilet

NO MATTER HOW GOOD YOU ARE, SOMETIMES YOU END UP WITH
A PLASTIC WATER BOTTLE. A good use for that plastic bottle is
to create a do-it-yourself toilet-tank water displacer.

Typically toilets use up to six gallons per flush. Sometimes this
information is listed at the base of the toilet behind the seat.
Here's how to make a DIY displacer to save some of those gallons.
Note that this only works for a toilet with a tank in the back.

Take an old water bottle, fill it with water, and place it in the tank
of your toilet. That's it! Congratulations, you have made your own
low-flow toilet. The amount of water that is displaced by the water
bottle is saved with each flush. Be careful not to
add too many water bottles, because displacing
too much water may affect the flushing quality
and mechanism. Start with one bottle, test it
out, and see if you want to add more to save
more water.

You can also purchase a water displacer.
These are sometimes called "Tank Banks"
because they save money! A water displacer
can easily be installed in any tank toilet and
knock gallons a day off your water bill. Water
displacers are not recommended for high-
efficiency toilets.

If you have a toilet with a tank like this one, try our
low-flow trick. Also, the flowers on the toilet tank
bring in life energy. Flowers (or a green plant) can
transform the downward water energy of the
bathroom into uplifting life energy.

BEDROOM

tip 74

There are many potential bedroom color palettes, depending on the person and life situation. The creamy whites and dreamy blues in this bedroom create a calming and restful place for you to rest and revitalize.

your bedroom represents you!

DID YOU KNOW YOUR BEDROOM ENVIRONMENT GREATLY INFLUENCES YOUR STRESS LEVELS AND ABILITY TO TRULY REST AND RESET? We spend many passive, yin hours sleeping in this room. In feng shui philosophy, your bedroom represents you. You can use feng shui to create a harmonious space of relaxation and repose.

In order to transform your bedroom into a soothing environment, it is important to relocate any stimulating objects. Books, electronics, and work items are often too energizing and engaging for the bedroom. In general, remove these sorts of items, as they may induce stress when you are trying to rest.

Soft hues of blues and greens are the most relaxing and healing colors for the bedroom because they suggest life. Greens and blues represent tranquility and healthy supportive energy. Think of the colors we often find in nature: big trees, the ocean, and the sky above. Feng shui recommends avoiding too much white, which can be stressful on the eyes (imagine being in a field of snow without sunglasses). Additionally, too much red or yellow is often overstimulating. These colors are better used for accents.

double up your bedroom objects

WHETHER YOU ARE IN A RELATIONSHIP OR LOOKING FOR A RELATIONSHIP, TAKE A LOOK AROUND YOUR BEDROOM. How many things are in pairs, and how many single objects are there? These objects are metaphors.

Photographs or artwork of a single person, and a single nightstand, count as singles. It is beneficial to have two nightstands, two bedside lamps, couples in photographs or art…do you see a trend? One great way to bring in that relationship energy is to purchase two new lucky bamboo stalks. Make sure they are straight and not the curly type. Straight bamboo represents upward and positive growth of similar and balanced partners. Place the two stalks together in a vase with water. This is about having pairs in unity.

If you are single, this means you are ready for an equal partner in your life and have made space for them. If you are in a relationship, it symbolizes a balanced and supportive relationship.

Doubling up can be as simple as having matching sets of pillows. Your partner (or future partner) should have a comfortable place to rest their head.

tip 76

location, location, location!

TAKE A LOOK AT WHERE THE BEDROOMS ARE LOCATED IN RELATIONSHIP
TO THE ENTRY DOOR OF YOUR ENTIRE HOME.

It is best to locate bedrooms for family members toward the back of
the residence. This places the inhabitants in a commanding position
of the space. If possible, the parents' room should be the furthest to
the rear, because this places them in the most control of the space.
If the child's room holds the furthest position from the front door, the
child might have power over the parents. Ideally, it should be the
reverse, where the parents are in charge.

If a family member has a bedroom very close to the front door, he or
she may feel easily divided from the rest of the family and spend less
time at home. Guest bedrooms are better suited closer to the entry of
the home, so your guests don't stay beyond their welcome.

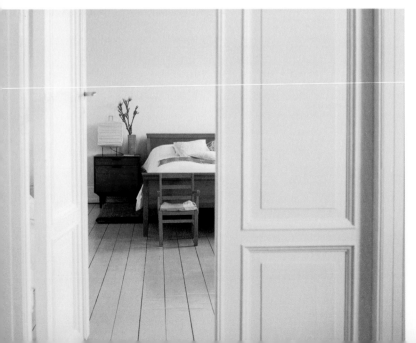

We spend so much passive time in
our bedrooms, they hold and
affect our qi. The location of our
bedroom also relates to the
natural hierarchy in the family.

twin? queen? king?

YES, THE SIZE OF YOUR BED DOES MATTER! But in this case, bigger is not always better. Twin beds are okay for children. They're even okay to push up against the wall if you have to. But a twin bed is not ideal for an adult that is in or would like to be in a romantic relationship. There is simply no room for anyone in your bed or in your life.

The king-sized bed, including the California king, is like having a vast desert separating you from your partner! Besides placing partners far apart, the box springs required for such large beds come as two separate pieces, creating a divide between the two partners. This is not conducive to a compatible and positive relationship.

It is better to get a bed that's comfortable, but with a single box spring. If that's not possible, you can put a piece of red fabric between the box springs and mattress to energetically repair the divide.

The bed is one thing you don't want a pair of in the bedroom! It's best to have one mattress and a single box spring base. You want to be connected to your partner (or future partner).

tip 78

a space for each partner

IF YOU ARE IN A RELATIONSHIP, AND ESPECIALLY IF YOU ARE LOOKING FOR ONE, THE IDEAL LOCATION FOR YOUR BED IS WITH THE HEAD AGAINST A WALL, AND THE FOOT OF THE BED OPEN TO THE CENTER OF THE ROOM WITH SPACE ON THE LEFT AND RIGHT SIDES. In other words, it is ideal to set up the bed so that there is clear and balanced open space on both sides.

There are two feng shui implications of having one side of the bed next to the wall. First, your qi will be unbalanced. It will be weaker on the side next to the wall, whether the weakness affects one side of your body or the person sleeping on the wall side. Second, if you are looking for a partner, by pushing the bed against the wall, you're not allowing space for someone to come into your life. If you are in a relationship, one person is more crammed in, which may represent an unbalanced dynamic in the relationship. One partner may feel more locked in or controlled. If the left or right side of your bed is pushed against a wall, this sends the universe the message that the balance of energy between you and your partner is not equal.

Open up the space on the left and right sides of the bed to invite a partner in if you're single. If you're in a relationship, make some space for each person to grow in harmony with the other; complementary yet, at the same time, individual.

update your bed linens based on your mood

SINCE WE SPEND MANY PASSIVE YIN HOURS ASLEEP IN BED, THE COLOR OF BED LINEN CAN GREATLY AFFECT MOOD AND ASSIST IN MANIFESTING CHANGE.

Although I like white linens, they are generally viewed as too metal, meaning too stark or harsh for a bedroom. If you love white like me, go for a soft ivory, or mix it up with some accent colors in your pillows or a throw.

If you're looking to spice things up, deep reds and purples are both great colors to invoke passion. Yellow is earthy and good for those who need more stability or support. Greens and blues are healing and relaxing colors. They may be helpful if you have trouble sleeping and feeling fully rested, while pink or peach is excellent for attracting a partner.

It's easy to update accessories like your bed linen, pillows, and lamps to support any of the five elements you'd like to invite into your life. You can even change the accents in the bedroom based on the seasons. Tap into what you need, and bring it in with the color, texture, and shapes of the five elements.

A solid and substantial headboard is essential for bedroom feng shui. It can offer support through the ups and downs in a relationship.

headboard for stability

I FIND THAT A LOT OF PEOPLE DON'T HAVE HEADBOARDS FOR THEIR BEDS. Headboards are so important for relationships in feng shui, because they represent stability and connectedness in a romantic relationship. Do you have a headboard? If not, maybe it's time to get one.

A solid and sturdy headboard is like a strong backbone for a relationship. Be sure the headboard is fastened securely to the bed, rather than attached to or casually leaning against the wall. When the headboard is not securely attached to the mattress, the stability that the headboard can provide is compromised.

In selecting the best feng shui headboard, choose something solid. A solid and stable headboard without major perforations is preferred. The shape is also important. Rectangular, rounded, and heart-shaped are all acceptable. Avoid bars or anything with many perforations, as that can feel like imprisonment or instability. There is not a huge difference between a solid wood and a soft upholstered headboard, as long as both partners are comfortable with the style. Remember, it is there to support both of you!

art in the bedroom

TAKE SOME TIME TO LOOK AT WHAT YOUR BEDROOM ARTWORK SYMBOLIZES.
The bedroom is a place of rest and relaxation. Any artwork that is tranquil
and nurturing in color and subject matter is ideal, especially if you have
trouble sleeping. Pale, muted, or dark blues, greens, pinks, and purples in
art can create a restful mood in a bedroom. If you want to bring in a little
more spice and passion, add red artwork to bring in some fire energy.

As far as imagery, feng shui encourages you to have things in pairs in the
bedroom. Pairs of images, whether they show people or objects that are
similar but not necessarily identical, give the universe the message that you
are open to or are currently in a partnership that is balanced and equal with
another person. I'm not just talking about images of couples, but perhaps
two similar pieces of art in similar frames.

Finally, are family photos or photos of Mom and Dad facing the bed? How
unsexy is it to have Mom, Dad, and/or a sibling staring at you while you're
getting romantic? A photo of you and your partner is okay. If possible, place
family photos in another part of your home.

The concentric circles in this art
piece are a simple image and an
excellent example of how to
creatively bring in pairs. The
symbol of a circle nods to unity,
harmony, and connection. The
circle can remind us there is no
beginning or end, that we can
trust our partners and ourselves
because we are all interdependent.

what's underneath?

WHAT IS UNDERNEATH YOUR BED INFLUENCES YOUR SLEEP
AND WELL-BEING. Our beds and bedrooms are tied closely
to our personal energy, because we spend a lot of passive
time in the bedroom sleeping, but we often forget to look
underneath the bed.

It is recommended that you keep nothing under your bed
so that the energy and qi can flow easily around you while
you sleep. We spend many idle hours asleep, and during
this time we are susceptible to the energies of any objects
beneath the bed. Clutter under the bed may symbolize
unacknowledged blocks in your personal life and
relationships. Therefore, what we sleep above affects us!

If you must have storage under your bed, stick with soft,
bed-related items such as linens, blankets, and pillows. Be
sure that there are no sharp objects and nothing negatively
nostalgic, like photos of ex-partners.

For emotional and physical health, it's recommended
to keep the area under the bed free and clear. We want
the qi to flow around us freely while we sleep.

a pair of nightstands

One reason why it's important to have two nightstands is so that each partner (or future partner) has a place of their own. Somewhere for a glass of water and whatever else is needed to rest. Matching is not required, just a balance.

IN FENG SHUI, IT IS VERY IMPORTANT TO HAVE SPACE ON BOTH SIDES OF YOUR BED, WITH A NIGHTSTAND ON EACH SIDE, TO SUPPORT AN EXISTING OR PROSPECTIVE ROMANTIC RELATIONSHIP. This is a way to let the universe know you have made a special space for an equal partner in your life.

The nightstands need not match exactly, but it is best when they are similar in dimension. Avoid extreme differences in size, which may indicate an imbalance in the relationship. If one nightstand is much larger and takes up more space, that may indicate an unbalanced power dynamic between the partners.

It is also a good idea to have a lamp for each partner. If you are looking to meet someone, the lamp adds fire energy. The fire calls attention to the space you have made available for your future partner.

If the headboard of your bed is against a wall shared with a bathroom or kitchen, take a closer look to see if you're sleeping with your head in line with a stove or toilet. If you are, you can hang a mirror above your bed. Make sure the mirror is in proportion to the bed. If it's a round mirror above the bed, it also promotes harmony in your partnership.

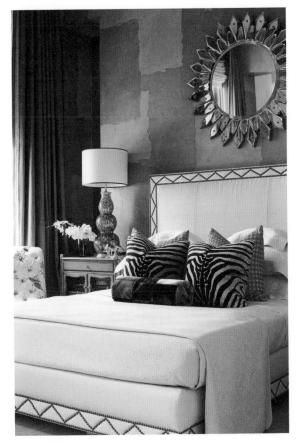

what is on the other side of your head?

WHEN LOCATING YOUR BED, TRY NOT TO PLACE THE HEAD OF YOUR BED NEXT TO A WALL WITH A TOILET OR STOVE ON THE OPPOSITE SIDE. This can cause a lot of problems for the person sleeping in that bed, including headaches and other health problems.

It's best to move the bed. If that's not possible, place a mirror on the wall over the bed to insulate the person from the flushing water energy of the toilet, or the heat and fire of the stove.

MEDITATION SPACE

DEFINE YOUR SPACE

DEDICATE AND CLEAR THE SPACE

ADD A BOWL OF WATER FOR CLARITY

tip 85

define your space

FENG SHUI IS A PHILOSOPHY DEVELOPED IN ANCIENT CHINA THAT OUTLINES POSITIVE WAYS IN WHICH TO ORGANIZE YOURSELF IN YOUR ENVIRONMENT. Meditation is a practice with which you can learn to become familiar with your inner landscape. Both feng shui and meditation are used to generate harmony and peace within your life. Why not use feng shui to create a sacred space in which to meditate that can support and improve your meditation practice?

Select a dedicated space that you can routinely go back to for your meditation practice. It can be the corner of your bed, a room in your home, or a place outside in your backyard. My meditation space is a quiet section of my living room that faces a river view. It is okay if you cannot find a perfectly quiet spot. Life is full of distractions, and part of meditation is to learn to accept the interruptions.

You can further differentiate your space by sitting on a special pillow, cushion, or blanket. I have a couple of buckwheat zafu cushions specifically designed for meditation. This can help you to dedicate and define your special spot.

Meditation, like feng shui, is about paying attention to the details of life and truly appreciating our inner and outer environments. Meditating in an area that connects us to nature can be a beautiful reminder to slow down and appreciate the phenomenal world around us.

Your meditation space can be anywhere—it may simply be a pillow in the living room. Take just a few moments to acknowledge and dedicate this place and meditation time in a mindful way to change the energy to support your practice. You can also use sunlight to clear your meditation space. Open up those windows and let in the sun, or even visualize bright sunlight filling your meditation area.

dedicate and clear the space

AFTER YOU HAVE SELECTED YOUR MEDITATION SPACE AND DEFINED IT PHYSICALLY, IT IS OF UTTER IMPORTANCE TO CLEAR AND DEDICATE THE AREA ENERGETICALLY. Space clearing dedicates the invisible energy of the space so you can start fresh and set your intention for the space, the particular moment, and your life.

In feng shui, oranges and orange peels represent vibrant, life-affirming energy. Orange essence is refreshing, happy, and contributes positive, fresh, and brightening energy to our inner and outer environments. You can use nine drops of orange essential oil in an aromatherapy diffuser to transform your area into a space with vibrant, life-giving, positive energy. Remember, when you clear the space of the existing energy, be sure to replace it with positive intention.

add a bowl of water for clarity

IN FENG SHUI, WATER CAN BE USED TO BRING CLARITY TO YOUR MEDITATION SPACE.
The element of water is often included in traditional meditation practices. To do this yourself, you can find a beautiful bowl or cup that you love. At the start of each practice session, humbly offer fresh water in your bowl or cup. The still water in the bowl can reflect your mind as it begins to settle down and find peace.

Water is a wonderful element to include when you create your own sacred meditation place, to promote harmony in your inner and outer spaces.

Water offerings signify clarity in a meditation space. A clear vase with beautiful foliage and blooms can bring joy and illuminating brilliance to your meditation practice.

CLOSETS

CLOSET SYMBOLISM

CREATE SPACE IN YOUR CLOSET

Many people have shared with me how happy they feel when they have an organized closet. See what happens when you give some TLC to a cluttered closet. You'll be surprised to discover how it uplifts your energy!

closet symbolism

TAKE A LOOK AT WHERE YOUR CLOSETS ARE LOCATED BASED ON THE BAGUA MAP. Take special note of which closets are cluttered or unused. Maybe you are afraid to open some of the closets because you need to go through them! These can represent hidden or unacknowledged issues.

For instance, an unused closet in the Benefactors area may represent helpful people that you have had in your life all along but have not yet tapped into or recognized. You just need to look and ask them for support. A cluttered closet in Abundance may indicate that your wealth is tied up or buried under personal issues or blocks.

If you have a closet in the feng shui area of Path in Life, maybe there's a path you have not yet seen. Are you open to seeing an alternate direction with your career? Or what about a closet in Relationships? Perhaps that relationship you want has been hard to find or hidden. Maybe you need to look a little deeper and open the door to a partner who was always there. And if you have a cluttered closet in Relationships, maybe it's time to de-clutter things and make some space for the love in your life.

It's interesting how our modern society is so... full! When we can let go of those "I'll fit into them someday" jeans, our hearts and minds will also open and release unwanted things like weight, stress, and harmful people. Try creating some space to invite new energy.

create space in your closet

FENG SHUI PRINCIPLES ENCOURAGE US TO PEEK INTO THOSE DARK CLOSETS, OPEN UP ALL THE WINDOWS, AND REALLY START SHIFTING THE ENERGY IN OUR SPACES. In feng shui, we seek to release stale, stuck energy and welcome in new, vibrant life energy.

Set aside a box for items that have not been worn in the last three years. If there are things that are in poor condition, you can donate those items to textile recycling. There are organizations that collect usable, as well as unusable, clothing and shoes. The unusable shoes and textiles can be made into rags or shredded and recycled for other uses.

Keep in mind that in feng shui, if your closet is full, you will not have room for anything new. This applies literally and metaphorically. If your closet is full, you will have no space to accept new opportunities. There is no room to grow. So, recycle anything that you don't need, and create a vacuum for the universe to bring something new and fantastic into your life.

PLANTS

add houseplants

DID YOU KNOW THAT HOUSEPLANTS IMPROVE THE OVERALL INDOOR AIR QUALITY IN YOUR HOME? While it's a well-known fact that plants convert carbon dioxide into oxygen through photosynthesis, many houseplants also remove harmful chemicals such as trichloroethylene, benzene, and formaldehyde from the air. They also add natural beauty to your home, bringing some nature indoors.

From the feng shui perspective, plants add the wood element: life energy and flexibility for the inhabitants of the home. They can create a softer and more vibrant energy in a home and are healing visually and physically.

The areca palm, mother-in-law's tongue, and the money plant all promote blood oxygenation; reduce headaches; reduce eye and respiratory irritation; increase human productivity; reduce energy costs; and add life energy.

Living green plants add the wood element and vitality into your home. They're especially feng shui-worthy in a bathroom, because they can transform the downward water energy into upward growing life qi.

tip 91

lucky bamboo

BAMBOO IS A PLANT THAT IS ABUNDANT IN ASIA AND GROWS VERY QUICKLY. In feng shui, it represents upright and honest growth as well as flexibility and adaptability. The bamboo plant does not flower or fruit—its lifespan is long but simple. It is also hollow, which represents an empty heart of humbleness. Coincidentally, in Western culture it is a symbol for the green (sustainability) movement.

In feng shui, bamboo is best when it is straight and not curly or twisted, which can represent the opposite of upright and positive growth. Bamboo represents the wood element of kindness, flexibility, and healing growth. Plants also add life energy to a space. Bamboo is great because it can thrive in a variety of lighting conditions, in water or in soil, and it's very easy to find.

If you're looking for more prosperity, you can place three or nine stalks in the Abundance area of your home, office, or bedroom—better yet, in all three locations. The bamboo will represent positive and steady growth.

A pair of plants, similar but slightly different, growing together in the same pot, can give support and harmony in your (current or future) partnerships—especially when located in the relationship area of your bedroom.

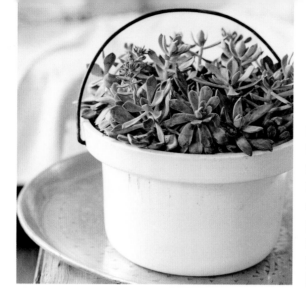

Not every plant in your home has to be a feng shui adjustment. However, when you purchase a new plant with the intention to use it as a feng shui adjustment, softer and rounder leaves are preferable. And remember, you can place it in a bagua area where you would like to see growth, new beginnings, and flexibility.

what to look for in houseplants

INDOOR TREES AND PLANTS PROVIDE POSITIVE LIFE ENERGY FOR HOME QI. But some types of plants are better than others.

As a rule of (green!) thumb, in feng shui we generally prefer plants with soft and rounded leaves. This shape offers a softer and gentler energy. Plants with sharp leaves, thorns, or spiky needles are best avoided for feng shui applications. If you have these in your home already, it's okay to keep them as long as they are healthy and well taken care of. For example, maybe you have a great attachment to a cactus that you received from your grandmother years ago. This is fine, but in general, if you want to add a plant to your home with a feng shui intention, go for something less prickly.

Always be sure to research the right plants for the type of daylight available in your selected space. A plant that is not suited for your indoor space will be challenging to care for and will not thrive, and that's just not good feng shui.

tip 93

No more dried flowers, and no more throwing out living orchid plants! Potted orchids are plants that can keep flowering after their first blooms have withered away. Simply cut off the dead flower and water the orchid plant sparingly. Orchids, especially in a bedroom, can attract an upright and noble partner.

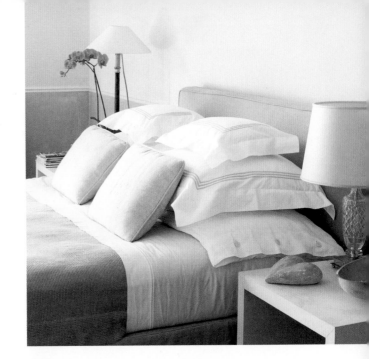

no more dried flowers

WHEN I WAS GROWING UP, I USED TO DRY FLOWERS AND USE THEM AS DECORATIONS IN MY HOME. Little did I know that in feng shui, dead flowers bring dead energy into a home. While fresh flowers symbolize joy and life energy, dried flowers represent the opposite: sadness and death. If possible, it's best to toss them into the compost bin. I love how composting organic material can turn waste into something productive.

Some of my clients have sentimental dried flowers, such as their wedding bouquets. As long as this does not have negative emotions attached to it, such as might come with a divorce, you can clear the bouquet as you would a secondhand object, and keep it! Place 27 drops of orange essential oil in a spray bottle and fill it with water. Spray this essence onto the dried flowers to clear away old energy and rejuvenate them with vibrant new energy.

fertilize with organic compost

Composting is nature's way of recycling to reduce waste and ensure that organic materials are returned to the earth. Produced using scraps from already-eaten food and other organic waste, compost is a natural fertilizer, balances pH, and improves soil content with nutrients that are vital for the growth of many plants, from food plants to pretty plants.

Chemical fertilizers often leave behind a wealth of heavy metals (such as lead, arsenic, and cadmium) that can build up over time. Overuse of chemical fertilizers can actually bring death to the soil, making it dependent on these same fertilizers, thus costing even more money over time. Composting skirts this issue entirely, as compost is composed only of organic materials.

Whether you use your own or purchase some from a local source, organic compost is a holistic way to "feed" your plants. Your plants will thrive and flourish!

Inviting plants into your home for feng shui purposes is about making the time to give them attention and care. What is it that this living being needs from us to thrive? It's that mindfulness that cultivates the positive qi in your life.

153

DOORS AND WINDOWS

There is a feng shui adjustment where you perform good deeds every day for a set number of days. The first time I practiced this adjustment, I noticed my good deed was to open doors for people. After 27 days of this, I realized by opening doors for others, I was really opening doors of opportunity for kindness toward myself.

all about doors and windows

IN FENG SHUI, DOORS REPRESENT THE MOUTH, AND WINDOWS REPRESENT THE EYES, OF THE INHABITANTS IN A HOME.

If you have squeaky, stuck, or otherwise problematic doors, they may represent challenges in communication. This is especially true for the entry door, as it sets the mood for your experience of your home. If you have a squeaky, "crying" door, it sets the tone for negativity every time you walk into your home. Get out the toolbox and oil any squeaky hinges, and repair any problematic doors.

In feng shui, windows represent the eyes of the people of the home. Therefore, windows should be kept in good repair and operable. Windows should be clear and easy to open, so you can feel seen and heard as well as nourished.

Finally, make sure that all doors can open fully to 90 degrees. That means no clutter behind the doors. Doors govern how qi comes into your space. If your doors cannot open fully, you're cutting off the amount of energy that could enter your space.

open the eyes of your space

WINDOWS ARE THE EYES OF YOUR SPACE. Make sure yours are clean!

Dirty and dusty windows can affect your ability to see and communicate with the world and represent a lack of clarity in your life. Take special care to wash them well inside and out, and make sure the frames are in good repair so you can open and close them easily. Your environment and your perspective become clearer, brighter, and more vibrant when you clean your windows.

Instead of using a toxic commercial glass cleaner, try a green option or make your own with one part vinegar for one part water, and substitute newsprint for paper towels.

Improve your outlook by maintaining clean windows. Trust me; it makes a huge impact and allows you to see your world with more clarity.

Sparkling clear and bright windows clarify our view of the world. We can see with our eyes open without being clouded by our perceptions and personal judgments. We can begin to glimpse the everyday magic and joy that surrounds us.

where are your secondary doors located?

A SECONDARY DOOR MAY BE A BACK OR SIDE DOOR THAT OPENS TO THE EXTERIOR AND IS USED AS AN ALTERNATIVE ENTRANCE, SUCH AS THE GARAGE DOOR OR SIDE DOOR. These secondary doors, depending on the location, may be positive or negative and are definitely something to pay attention to.

Using the bagua map, the best location for a secondary door is in the Benefactors area, because it may indicate additional helpful people to support you in your life.

Locations to be concerned about would be in Relationships, where it may mean that there are extra marital partners or affairs in a relationship.

Also watch out for a back door in Abundance or Recognition. Your wealth or fame may leak out of this additional door. In both of these situations, the most ideal adjustment is to place a bell or chime on this door. The bell or chime symbolizes an alarm that will sound to alert the members of the household of any danger.

A bell—or something that makes a bit of noise—hung from the interior side door knob can adjust a secondary door. This is also useful if you are not in the commanding position of the room!

If you have three doorways in a row, it is best to hang feng shui faceted crystal balls halfway between each door to break up the qi.

piercing heart doors

IN FENG SHUI, IT IS IMPORTANT TO WATCH OUT FOR THREE OR MORE DOORWAYS IN A ROW. These are called "piercing heart doors." Open doorways without a door are also included in this definition of "doorway."

We need to watch out for this issue, because it can cause heart-related problems, physically and metaphorically. There is a feeling of contraction then openness, contraction then openness, and contraction and openness again. The feng shui remedy for this is to hang a feng shui faceted crystal ball from the ceiling between each doorway. For instance, if there are three doorways, you would hang two crystals in total (one between each pair of doorways). If there were four doors in a row, there would be three crystals. Each crystal must be strung on a red string long enough for the crystal to align with the top of each door header, without hitting the door when it swings out.

Use a feng shui crystal that is a minimum of ¼ inch (40 mm) in diameter. Since the crystals are multifaceted, just like with sunlight, they take the harmful energy and disperse it so that it is more gentle on your life and the energy of your home.

THE HOLISTIC HOME

NINE MINUTES A DAY KEEPS THE FENG SHUI
MASTER AWAY!

ELIMINATE EMFS

SWITCH TO A GREEN ENERGY PROVIDER

REPAIR OR TOSS ANYTHING BROKEN

TURN OFF UNNECESSARY LIGHTS AND
ELECTRICAL DEVICES

MIRRORS IN THE HOME

PLUG INTO POWER STRIPS

HEALTHY PAINT

UPLIFT YOUR HOME WITH ARTWORK

LOVE YOUR HOME!

tip 99

One way to minimize clutter is to make sure you have enough closed storage where you can organize the things that you do need. The visual calmness of a closet or cabinet door works wonders to decrease your stress levels.

nine minutes a day keeps the feng shui master away!

PRETTY MUCH EVERYONE IN THE WESTERN WORLD HAS CLUTTER. WE HAVE A LOT OF "STUFF." Stuff is a modern-day problem. It is not necessarily bad or good, but it may represent and cause blocks or stuck energy in your home and your life. That pile of magazines collecting dust in the living room may not only be an eyesore but also a constant reminder of another thing to clean. Or another item on the to-do list. Or even a source of guilt. It takes a lot of energy to ignore that clutter!

Please do not be too hard on yourself if you do have clutter; take it step by step. Start with the easy items that you know you no longer want. I suggest you start with nine minutes a day. Set an egg timer, and just do nine minutes of clutter clearing, then feel good about it!

To be clear, clutter is not always negative. It is okay as long as it doesn't hinder your life or cause guilt and distress. But it may be a problem if it prevents you from achieving your goals and leaves you feeling stuck.

eliminate EMFs

IN THE MODERN WORLD, WE ARE INUNDATED BY DANGEROUS ELECTROMAGNETIC FIELDS (EMFS) AND RADIATION EMITTED BY ELECTRONIC DEVICES SUCH AS WI-FI, PHONES, COMPUTERS, AND EVEN THE ELECTRICAL WIRING IN OUR HOMES. EMFs produce stress in the body and cause health problems such as fatigue, headaches, and even nausea.

If possible, I encourage you to reduce the number of electronic devices in your home. An easy place to start is in the bedroom, where EMFs affect you during passive sleep time. Simply unplug or remove unnecessary devices. It is recommended that any electronics (including extension cords and any other cords or charging devices) remain a minimum of 5 ft (1.5 m) away from where you sleep. Battery-operated devices are fine.

A secondary benefit is that you will reduce your energy use and costs, making your home not only healthier, but also greener.

Set any electronic devices on airplane mode with the wi-fi off if they must be near the bed. A small plant or a vase of flowers on the nightstand can help to neutralize the energy of any EMFS.

switch to a green energy provider

AN EASY WAY TO MINIMIZE YOUR CARBON FOOTPRINT IS TO SWITCH TO A RENEWABLE ENERGY PROVIDER. Switching to green power does not typically mean that you need to install solar panels or a windmill on your roof. Although that is sometimes an option, in most urban areas you can simply call your electricity provider and request to be switched to a green or renewable energy source. You may see a small increase in your monthly bill, but in my experience it is very minimal.

Signing up for renewable energy will help your home substantially reduce its carbon footprint through the use of wind, solar power, or other renewable sources. If applicable in your state or country, your energy company will still deliver your electricity, but they will buy your power from a company that creates energy sustainably. You can also look into Renewable Energy Certificates (RECs) to offset your "dirty" electricity usage.

We have more and more computers, appliances, electronics, and gadgets in our everyday lives. They are all tools that help us, but we can make wiser and more sustainable choices for the future by upgrading to renewable energy.

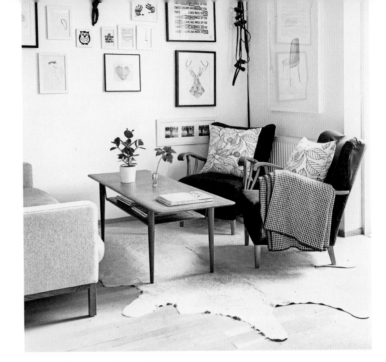

repair or toss anything broken

YOU KNOW THAT OLD LAMP YOU HAVE BEEN MEANING TO FIX? BROKEN THINGS MAY REPRESENT WEAKENED ENERGY. They can also be a guilty and constant reminder of something that you "should" do.

A broken doorbell may be hindering your chances of getting a new job or meeting a new person. A stove in disrepair may represent a block in your wealth and nourishment. Even that burned-out light bulb in your desk lamp needs to be replaced. It may prevent you from coming up with some bright ideas in your career.

What's stopping you from repairing that object? If it is important to you, get it repaired, or give it away to someone who can. Don't let that stuck energy stop you from moving forward in life.

A broken chair in the living room is not only dangerous for someone that could sit on it, but may represent an area of your life that needs some attention and support. Repairing a chair in need may invite deeper friendships into your life.

Every living thing yearns for more light. The sun provides warmth and energy. Take some time each day to use as much daylight as you can. When selecting window treatments, install drape panels so that they don't actually block the window. You'll be able to let in more daylight and the window will look wider.

turn off unnecessary lights and electrical devices

CONSIDER TURNING OFF SOME LIGHTS IN YOUR HOME DURING THE DAY OR ALTOGETHER TO SAVE ENERGY. An easy way to incorporate this is to upgrade to a light switch with an occupancy sensor. That means that when you leave the room, the light will turn off automatically. This can be effective in areas like basements and bathrooms.

Use natural daylight, which is better for your mood, for the earth, and for your budget! Even if you leave the room for only a few minutes, you save energy and money by turning off the lights.

tip 104

In feng shui, mirrors can energetically and visually work with our spaces. In this case, if your dining table is located close to your front door, it may mean it's more challenging to cultivate deep friendships. The reflection of the table in the mirror can pull the dining area back, away from the front door, correcting the feng shui.

mirrors in the home

MIRRORS ARE USED FREQUENTLY AS FENG SHUI ADJUSTMENT OBJECTS TO TWEAK SITUATIONS THAT ARE LESS THAN IDEAL. Mirrors can add water energy, expand your view, eliminate negative energy, and add positive qi. They are often used to adjust your view and put you back in the commanding position.

Mirrors are particularly useful for any weak or missing areas of the feng shui bagua map. If you lay the bagua map on your space and there is a missing or weak area, placing a mirror facing into your home (with the back facing the missing or weak area) will help to expand and take back some of that area. Mirrors can also be used to make up for any missing area.

Be sure the mirrors are not broken or jagged. Mosaic mirrors or mirrors that are divided up are not appropriate for feng shui applications because they promote disjointed energy.

plug into power strips

USE POWER STRIPS, AND TURN THEM OFF WHEN NOT IN USE. You can purchase power strips at any hardware store for very little money.

A lot of electronics, especially those with any sort of standby light, continue to draw energy although they appear to be off. This is called "vampire power." On average, 40 percent of electricity used to power home electronics is consumed while the products are turned off but still plugged in. When plugged in but not on, all appliances draw a phantom load equal to 30 percent of their full load.

If you plug electronics into a power strip and then turn off the strip when you are not using them, you can ensure they will no longer draw on electricity when turned off. This may be helpful for appliances, printers, DVD players, and other peripheral devices, including televisions and gaming systems.

Important note: for significant energy savings, turn off your power strips when you leave your home.

If you go away for a few days, it saves energy to simply turn off your electronics. If you aren't going away, set your computer to go to sleep when it's not in use to save electricity. Mindfulness goes beyond just meditation; it's also about how we look at all the details in our life.

tip 106

Even the smallest splash of paint on the wall can transform the experience of a space. Another fun option is to purchase a very large blank canvas and paint it a single color. It doesn't have to be a dramatically vivid hue, unless that's what you want. You can look to the five element colors to bring some complementary energies into your home.

healthy paint

THE SIMPLEST WAY TO REDEFINE AN AREA IS WITH PAINT COLORS. This is a fairly easy and inexpensive way to change up the way your home looks and feels. But no matter what color you choose, the type of paint you use can make a difference.

The green option is a low- or zero-VOC (volatile organic compound) paint. VOCs are chemicals added to paint for a variety of reasons, including color enhancement, increased adhesiveness, and increased ease of spreading. Despite these conveniences, VOCs are extremely dangerous to humans, and the use of them in many paints results in indoor air being anywhere from three to five times more polluted and harmful than outdoor air. Traditional paints have VOCs, which release toxins into the air for years after the paint is applied. In no way is that good for anyone in your home.

Today, many paint companies offer low- or zero-VOC options. In addition to the long-term benefits in terms of air quality, they have minimal odor when wet! There are even zero-VOC food-based paints made with milk casein.

Your choice of artwork is deeply personal, so go with what soothes and heals you. A picture frame ledge like this one allows for flexibility to update and change your artwork. Another benefit is that it can keep the qi in your home moving as you switch up the images.

uplift your home with artwork

ARTWORK IS A GREAT, HOLISTIC WAY TO UPLIFT THE ENERGY OF YOUR HOME. Art can bring in beauty as well as positive qi.

First of all, we can look at subject matter. Choosing artwork is really a matter of personal preference, but something optimistic and uplifting is generally more positive than something dark and depressing. That said, go with what makes you feel good inside.

Also, look at where the art came from. You might have pieces that have been passed down to you. What is the predecessor energy attached to the art? Is it helpful or harmful to you? If necessary, do some energy clearings to really make the art your own.

Finally, make sure the height of the artwork is appropriate for the area it is in. While it depends on the situation, a good rule of thumb is for the artwork to be at a standing person's eye level or higher. Artwork that is too low may bring down your energy levels.

tip 108

Feng shui gives us tools to slow down and create a home that supports and nurtures us. This world we live in is beautiful and it takes just a little mindfulness to appreciate all the details in our homes and our lives.

love your home!

HERE WE ARE AT NUMBER 108, MY FINAL TIP TO CREATE HOLISTIC SPACES!

You have learned 107 ways to create holistic spaces that support and nurture you and your loved ones. As you incorporate these tips into your home, remember: It is your home, so your energy, and your intentions, are key.

Each time you try a feng shui adjustment, pay attention to how it feels to you. Does the shape or color or object placement feel good to you? If not, try a few subtle shifts until it does.

You want to look around your space and love the way it looks and feels. The more you do, the more these adjustments, and your home as a whole, will serve you.

Whatever you desire for your space and your life, bring love and intention to it. When you love your home, you will truly be living in a holistic space that supports and nurtures you and your loved ones.

"Om mani padme hum—the jewel is in the lotus."
—Sanskrit mantra

index

photography credits

Front cover: **Mark Scott**
Back cover: **Paul Massey** (center); **Debi Treloar** (right)

Polly Wreford: p.1, 5, 10, 17, 21, 24, 52, 70, 84 (right), 88, 89, 100, 105, 107, 110, 117, 119, 120, 125, 128, 141 (bottom), 145, 154, 160, 167 (right), 172
Simon Brown: 2, 3, 13, 26, 35 (right), 40, 51, 54, 66, 68, 84 (center), 99, 114, 157, 158
William Reavell: 4, 7, 36, 41, 44, 61, 65, 82, 86, 136, 146, 166
Paul Massey: 9, 20, 30, 112
Jo Henderson: 16, 35 (center right), 47 (top)
Henry Bourne: 18
James Gardiner: 19, 106
Mark Scott: 22, 29, 47 (bottom), 74, 162
Debi Treloar: 28, 31 (bottom), 33, 58 (left), 58 (right), 59, 62, 69, 92, 94
Emma Mitchell: 34, 46, 73, 97, 121, 163
Andrew Wood: 38
Earl Carter: 43, 56, 122
Rachel Whiting: 48, 116, 129, 142, 156, 165, 168
Christopher Drake: 50, 87, 152, 164
Richard Jung: 55
Jan Baldwin: 60, 67, 72, 80, 93, 127, 134, 135, 167 (left)
Claire Richardson: 64, 75
Catherine Gratwicke: 79, 153, 169
Caroline Arber: 85, 111 (left)
Kate Whitaker: 90 (left)
Mark Lohman: 90 (right)
Chris Tubbs: 91
Winfried Heinze: 96
Helen Cathcart: 103, 149
Sandra Lane: 140
David Brittain: 141 (top)
Francesca Yorke: 150
Philip Webb: 151

Every effort has been made to contact copyright holders and acknowledge sources. Any omissions will be rectified in future printings, if brought to the publisher's attention.

Steven Post's Geomancy/Feng Shui Education Association can be found at geofengshui.com
email: geofs@pacbell.net

ACKNOWLEDGMENTS

I would like to thank my teachers, who have made this book possible: the late His Holiness Master Lin Yun, Rosalie Prinzivalli, Barry Gordon, and especially Steven Post for his many hours reading and advising me on the manuscript.

Thank you also for teaching me that I am a treasure, the jewel in the lotus. Om Mani Padme Hum.